California Common Core State Standards

English Language Arts & Literacy in History/Social Studies, Science, and Technical Subjects

Adopted by the California State Board of Education
August 2010 and modified March 2013

Publishing Information

Senate Bill 1200, Statutes of 2012, provided for an update of the California Common Core State Standards: English Language Arts and Literacy in History/Social Studies, Science, and Technical Subjects (CA CCSS for ELA/Literacy). The CA CCSS for ELA/Literacy were modified on March 13, 2013, following the recommendation of State Superintendent of Public Instruction Tom Torlakson, to include the addition of the College and Career Readiness Anchor Standards and technical changes. When the CA CCSS for ELA/Literacy were modified, the members of the State Board of Education (SBE) were the following: Michael W. Kirst, President; Ilene Straus, Vice President; Sue Burr; Carl A. Cohn; Bruce Holaday; Josephine Kao; Aida Molina; Patricia Ann Rucker; Nicolasa Sandoval; and Trish Boyd Williams.

Senate Bill 1 from the fifth Extraordinary Session (SB X5 1) in 2010 established the California Academic Content Standards Commission (Commission) to evaluate the Common Core State Standards for English Language Arts and Literacy in History/Social Studies, Science, and Technical Subjects developed by the Common Core State Standards Initiative for rigor and alignment with the California standards. Based on the evaluation, the Commission inserted words, phrases, and select California standards to maintain California's high expectations for students. On July 15, 2010, the Commission recommended that the SBE adopt the CA CCSS for ELA/Literacy as amended. The members of the Commission were the following: Greg Geeting, Chair; Heather Calahan; Steven Dunlap; Robert Ellis; Eleanor Evans; Bill Evers; Scott Farrand; Mark Freathy; Lori Freiermuth; Bruce Grip; Kathy Harris; Jeanne Jelnick; Deborah Keys; James Lanich; Matt Perry; Pat Sabo; Brian Shay; Alba Sweeney; Hilda Villarreal Writ; Chuck Weis; and Ze'ev Wurman. Support for the Commission was provided by the Sacramento County Office of Education under the direction of Sue Stickel, Deputy Superintendent of Schools.

When the CA CCSS for ELA/Literacy were adopted by the SBE on August 2, 2010, the members of the SBE were the following: Theodore Mitchell, President; Ruth Bloom, Vice President; Alan Arkatov; James Aschwanden; Benjamin Austin; Yvonne Chan; Gregory Jones; David Lopez; and Johnathan Williams. Jack O'Connell, former State Superintendent of Public Instruction, is also recognized for his leadership during the adoption of the standards in August 2010.

The *California Common Core State Standards: English Language Arts and Literacy in History/Social Studies, Science, and Technical Subjects* was edited in part by the staff of CDE Press, with the cover and interior design prepared by Tuyet Truong. It was published by the California Department of Education, 1430 N Street, Sacramento, CA 95814-5901. It was distributed under the provisions of the Library Distribution Act and *Government Code* Section 11096. The Common Core State Standards appear as they were published by the Common Core State Standards Initiative.

Special Acknowledgments

Special appreciation is extended to Tom Torlakson, State Superintendent of Public Instruction, for support of the revision and update of the CA CCSS for ELA/Literacy. Special commendation is extended to Lupita Cortez Alcalá, Deputy Director, Instruction and Learning Support Branch; Thomas Adams, Director, Curriculum Frameworks and Instructional Resources Division; Kristen Cruz Allen, Administrator, and Cynthia Gunderson, Consultant, Curriculum Frameworks Unit.

Special recognition is awarded to Joy Kessel, Analyst, Common Core Systems Implementation Office, for her contribution to the original organization and format design.

Ordering Information

Copies of the *California Common Core State Standards: English Language Arts and Literacy in History/Social Studies, Science, and Technical Subjects* are available for purchase from the California Department of Education. For prices and ordering information, please visit the Department Web site at http://www.cde.ca.gov/re/pn/rc or call the CDE Press Sales Office at 1-800-995-4099.

Notice

Contents

The first academic content standards for English language arts adopted by California in 1997 set a bold precedent—the establishment of a statewide, standards-based education system to improve academic achievement and define what students should learn.

The commitment to a high-quality education, based on sound content standards, was reaffirmed in August 2010 when California joined with 45 other states and adopted the California Common Core State Standards: English Language Arts and Literacy in History/Social Studies, Science, and Technical Subjects (CA CCSS for ELA/Literacy). The CA CCSS for ELA/Literacy build on the rigor of the state's previous English language arts standards, incorporating current research and input from other educational sources—including state departments of education, scholars, professional organizations, teachers and other educators, parents, and students. Also, California additions to the standards (identified in bold typeface and "CA," the state abbreviation) were incorporated in an effort to retain the consistency and precision of our past standards. The CA CCSS for ELA/Literacy are rigorous, based on research and evidence, and internationally benchmarked. They address the demands of today to prepare students to succeed tomorrow.

The CA CCSS for ELA/Literacy are organized around a number of key design considerations. The College and Career Readiness anchor standards constitute the backbone of the standards and define the general, cross-disciplinary literacy expectations for students in preparation for college and the workforce. The standards are divided into strands: Reading, Writing, Speaking and Listening, and Language. Connected to these design considerations is the interdisciplinary expectation that the development of each student's literacy skills is a shared responsibility—English language arts teachers collaborating with teachers of other academic content subjects for an integrated model of literacy across the curriculum.

The standards establish what it means to be a literate person in the twenty-first century. Students learn to closely read and analyze critical works of literature and an array of nonfiction text in an exploding print and digital world. They use research and technology to sift through the staggering amount of information available and engage in collaborative conversations, sharing and reforming viewpoints through a variety of written and speaking applications. Teachers, schools, districts, and county offices of education are encouraged to use these standards to design specific curricular and instructional strategies that best deliver the content to their students.

The CA CCSS for ELA/Literacy help build creativity and innovation, critical thinking and problem solving, collaboration, and communication. They set another bold precedent to improve the academic achievement of California's students. The standards develop the foundation for creative and purposeful expression in language—fulfilling California's vision that all students graduate from our public school system as lifelong learners and have the skills and knowledge necessary to be ready to assume their position in our global economy.

Michael W. Kirst

MICHAEL W. KIRST, President
California State Board of Education

Tom Torlakson

TOM TORLAKSON
State Superintendent of Public Instruction

Introduction

Introduction

The Common Core State Standards for English Language Arts & Literacy in History/Social Studies, Science, and Technical Subjects (hereafter referred to as "the Standards") are the culmination of an extended, broad-based effort to fulfill the charge issued by the states to create the next generation of standards in kindergarten to grade 12 to help ensure that all students are literate and college and career ready no later than the end of high school.

The present work, led by the Council of Chief State School Officers (CCSSO) and the National Governors Association (NGA), builds on the foundation laid by states in their decades-long work on crafting high-quality education standards. The Standards also draw on the most important international models as well as research and input from numerous sources, including state departments of education, scholars, assessment developers, professional organizations, educators from kindergarten through college, and parents, students, and other members of the public. In design and content, through successive drafts and numerous rounds of feedback, the Standards represent a synthesis of the best elements of standards-related work to date and an important advance over that previous work.

As specified by the CCSSO and NGA, the Standards are (1) based on research and evidence, (2) aligned with college and work expectations, (3) rigorous, and (4) internationally benchmarked. A particular standard was included in the document only when the best available evidence indicated that its mastery was essential for college and career readiness in a twenty-first-century, globally competitive society. The Standards are intended to be a living work: as new and better evidence emerges, the Standards will be revised accordingly.

The Standards are an extension of a prior initiative led by the CCSSO and NGA to develop College and Career Readiness (CCR) standards in reading, writing, speaking, listening, and language as well as in mathematics. The CCR Reading, Writing, and Speaking and Listening Standards (released in draft form in September 2009), serve, in revised form, as the backbone of the present document. Grade-specific K–12 standards in reading, writing, speaking, listening, and language translate the broad (and, for the earliest grades, seemingly distant) aims of the CCR standards into attainable and age-appropriate terms.

The Standards set requirements not only for English language arts (ELA) but also for literacy in history/social studies, science, and technical subjects. Just as students must learn to read, write, speak, listen, and use language effectively in a variety of content areas, so too must the Standards specify the literacy skills and understandings required for college and career readiness in multiple disciplines. Literacy standards for grade 6 and above are based on the expectation that teachers of ELA, history/social studies, science, and technical subjects use their expertise to help students meet the particular challenges of reading, writing, speaking, listening, and language in those content areas. It is important to note that the grades 6–12 literacy standards in history/social studies, science, and technical subjects are not meant to replace content standards in those areas but rather to supplement them. States may incorporate these standards into their standards for those subjects or adopt them as literacy standards in content areas.

As a natural outgrowth of meeting the charge to define college and career readiness, the Standards also lay out a vision of what it means to be a literate person in the twenty-first century. Indeed, the skills and understandings students are expected to demonstrate have wide application outside the classroom or workplace. Students who meet the Standards readily undertake the close, attentive reading that is at the heart of understanding and enjoying complex works of literature. They habitually perform the critical reading necessary to pick carefully through the staggering amount of information available today in print and digitally. They actively seek wide, deep, and thoughtful engagement with high-quality literary and informational texts that builds knowledge, enlarges experience, and broadens worldviews. They reflexively demonstrate cogent reasoning and use evidence in a way that is essential to both private deliberation

and responsible citizenship in a democratic republic. In short, students who meet the Standards develop the skills in reading, writing, speaking, and listening that are the foundation for any creative and purposeful expression in language.
June 2, 2010

Key Design Considerations

CCR and grade-specific standards

The CCR standards anchor and define general, cross-disciplinary literacy expectations that must be met for students to be prepared to enter college and workforce training programs ready to succeed. The K–12 grade-specific standards define end-of-year expectations and a cumulative progression designed to enable students to meet college- and career-readiness expectations no later than the end of high school. The CCR and high school (i.e., grades 9–12) standards work in tandem to define the college and career readiness baseline—the former providing broad standards, the latter providing additional specificity. Hence, both should be considered when college and career readiness assessments are developed.

Students advancing through the grades are expected to meet each year's standards for the grade level, retain or further develop skills and understandings mastered in preceding grades, and work steadily toward meeting the more general expectations described by the CCR standards.

Grade levels for K–8; grade bands for 9–10 and 11–12

The Standards are divided into individual grade levels in kindergarten through grade 8 to be more useful. Two-year bands are used for grades 9–10 and 11–12 to allow schools, districts, and states flexibility in high school course design.

A focus on results rather than means

By emphasizing required achievements, the Standards leave room for teachers, curriculum developers, and states to determine how the standards should be reached and what additional topics should be addressed. Thus, the Standards do not mandate such things as a particular writing process or the full range of metacognitive strategies that students may need to monitor and direct their thinking and learning. Teachers are therefore free to provide students with whatever tools and knowledge that professional judgment and experience deem to be most helpful for meeting the Standards.

An integrated model of literacy

Although the Standards are divided into Reading, Writing, Speaking and Listening, and Language strands for conceptual clarity, the processes of communication are closely intertwined, as reflected throughout this document. For example, Writing standard 9 requires that students be able to write about what they read. Likewise, Speaking and Listening standard 4 sets the expectation that students will share findings from their research.

Research and media skills blended into the Standards as a whole

To be ready for college, workforce training, and life in a technological society, students need the ability to gather, comprehend, evaluate, synthesize, and summarize information and ideas, to conduct original research to answer questions or solve problems, and to analyze and create a high volume and extensive range of print and nonprint texts in media forms old and new. The need to conduct research and to produce and consume media is embedded into every aspect of today's curriculum. In like fashion, research and media skills and understandings are embedded in the Standards rather than treated in a separate section.

Shared responsibility for students' literacy development

The Standards insist that instruction in reading, writing, speaking, listening, and language be a shared responsibility within the school. The K–5 standards include expectations for reading, writing, speaking, listening, and language applicable to a range of subjects, including but not limited to ELA. The grades 6–12 standards are divided into two sections: one for ELA and the other for history/social studies, science, and technical subjects. This division reflects the unique, time-honored place of ELA teachers in developing students' literacy skills while at the same time recognizing that teachers of other subjects must have a role in this development as well.

Part of the motivation behind the interdisciplinary approach to literacy promulgated by the Standards is extensive research establishing the need for college and career ready students to be proficient in reading complex informational text independently in a variety of content areas. Most of the required reading in college and in workforce training programs is informational in structure and challenging in content; postsecondary education programs typically provide students with both a higher volume of such reading than is generally required in K–12 schools and comparatively little scaffolding.

The Standards are not alone in calling for a special emphasis on informational text. The 2009 reading framework of the National Assessment of Educational Progress (NAEP) requires a high and increasing proportion of informational text on its assessment as students advance through the grades.

Distribution of Literary and Informational Passages by Grade in the 2009 NAEP Reading Framework

Grade	Literary	Informational
4	50%	50%
8	45%	55%
12	30%	70%

Source: National Assessment Governing Board. 2008. Reading Framework for the 2009 National Assessment of Educational Progress. Washington, DC: U.S. Government Printing Office.

The Standards aim to align instruction with this framework so that many more students than at present can meet the requirements of college and career readiness. In K–5, the Standards follow the NAEP's lead in balancing the reading of literature with the reading of informational texts, including texts in history/social studies, science, and technical subjects. In accord with the NAEP's growing emphasis on informational texts in the higher grades, the Standards demand that a significant amount of informational texts be read in and outside the ELA classroom. Fulfilling the Standards for grades 6–12 ELA requires much greater attention to a specific category of informational text—literary nonfiction—than has been traditional. Because the ELA classroom must focus on literature (e.g., stories, drama, and poetry) as well as literary nonfiction, a great deal of informational reading in grades 6–12 must take place in other classes if the NAEP assessment framework is to be matched instructionally.[1] To measure students' growth toward college and career readiness, assessments aligned with the Standards should adhere to the distribution of texts across grades cited in the NAEP framework.

NAEP likewise outlines a distribution across the grades of the core purposes and types of student writing. The 2011 NAEP framework, like the Standards, cultivates the development of three mutually reinforcing writing capacities: writing to persuade, to explain, and to convey real or imagined experience. Evidence concerning the demands of college and career readiness gathered during development of the Standards concurs with NAEP's shifting emphases: standards for grades 9–12 describe writing in all three forms, but, consistent with NAEP, the overwhelming focus of writing throughout high school should focus mostly on arguments and informative/explanatory texts.[2]

Distribution of Communicative Purposes by Grade in the 2011 NAEP Writing Framework

Grade	To Persuade	To Explain	To Convey Experience
4	30%	35%	35%
8	35%	35%	30%
12	40%	40%	20%

Source: National Assessment Governing Board. 2010. Writing Framework for the 2011 National Assessment of Educational Progress (Prepublication edition). Washington, DC: National Assessment Governing Board.

It follows that writing assessments aligned with the Standards should adhere to the distribution of writing purposes across grades outlined by the NAEP.

Focus and coherence in instruction and assessment

While the Standards delineate specific expectations in reading, writing, speaking and listening, and language, each standard need not be a separate focus for instruction and assessment. Often, several standards can be addressed by a single rich task. For example, when editing writing, students address Writing standard 5 ("Develop and strengthen writing as needed by planning, revising, editing, rewriting, or trying a new approach") as well as Language standards 1–3 (which deal with conventions of standard English and knowledge of language). When drawing evidence from literary and informational texts per Writing standard 9,

---

1. The percentages on the table reflect the sum of student reading, not just reading in ELA settings. Teachers of senior English classes, for example, are not required to devote 70 percent of reading to informational texts. Rather, 70 percent of student reading across the grade should be informational.

---

2. As with reading, the percentages in the table reflect the sum of student writing, not just writing in ELA settings.

students are also demonstrating their comprehension skill in relation to specific standards in Reading. When discussing something they have read or written, students are also demonstrating their speaking and listening skills. The CCR anchor standards themselves provide another source of focus and coherence.

The same ten CCR anchor standards for Reading apply to both literary and informational texts, including texts in history/social studies, science, and technical subjects. The ten CCR anchor standards for Writing cover numerous text types and subject areas. This means that students can develop mutually reinforcing skills and exhibit mastery of standards for reading and writing across a range of texts and classrooms.

What is not covered by the Standards

The Standards should be recognized for what they are not as well as what they are. The most important intentional design limitations are as follows:

1. The Standards define what all students are expected to know and be able to do, not how teachers should teach. For instance, the use of play with young children is not specified by the Standards, but it is welcome as a valuable activity in its own right and as a way to help children meet the expectations in this document. Furthermore, while the Standards make references to some particular forms of content, including mythology, foundational U.S. documents, and Shakespeare, they do not—indeed, cannot—enumerate all or even most of the content that students should learn. The Standards must therefore be complemented by a well-developed, content-rich curriculum consistent with the expectations laid out in this document.

2. While the Standards focus on what is most essential, they do not describe all that can or should be taught. A great deal is left to the discretion of teachers and curriculum developers. The aim of the Standards is to articulate the fundamentals, not to set out an exhaustive list or a set of restrictions that limits what can be taught beyond what is specified herein.

3. The Standards do not define the nature of advanced work for students who meet the Standards prior to the end of high school. For those students, advanced work in such areas as literature, composition, language, and journalism should be available. This work should provide the next logical step up from the college and career readiness baseline established here.

4. The standards set grade-specific standards but do not define the intervention methods or materials necessary to support students who are well below or well above grade-level expectations. No set of grade-specific standards can fully reflect the great variety in abilities, needs, learning rates, and achievement levels of students in any given classroom. However, the Standards do provide clear signposts along the way to the goal of college and career readiness for all students.

5. It is also beyond the scope of the Standards to define the full range of supports appropriate for English language learners and for students with special needs. At the same time, all students must have the opportunity to learn and meet the same high standards if they are to acquire the knowledge and skills necessary in their post–high school lives.

   Each grade will include students who are still acquiring English. For those students, it is possible to meet the standards in reading, writing, speaking, and listening without displaying native-like control of conventions and vocabulary.

   The Standards should also be read as allowing the widest possible range of students to participate fully from the outset and as permitting appropriate accommodations to ensure maximum participation by students with special education needs. For example, for students with disabilities *reading* should allow for the use of Braille, screen-reader technology, or other assistive devices, while *writing* should include the use of a scribe, computer, or speech-to-text technology. In a similar vein, *speaking* and *listening* should be interpreted broadly to include the use of sign language.

6. While the ELA and content area literacy components described herein are critical to college and career readiness, they do not define the whole of such readiness. Students require a wide-ranging, rigorous academic preparation and, particularly in the early grades, attention to such matters as social, emotional, and physical development and approaches to learning. Similarly, the Standards define literacy expectations in history/social studies, science, and technical subjects, but literacy standards in other areas, such as mathematics and health education, modeled on those in this document are strongly encouraged to facilitate a comprehensive, schoolwide literacy program.

Students Who Are College and Career Ready in Reading, Writing, Speaking and Listening, and Language

The descriptions that follow are not standards themselves but instead offer a portrait of students who meet the standards set out in this document. As students advance through the grades and master the standards in reading, writing, speaking and listening, and language, they exhibit, with increasing fullness and regularity, the following capabilities of the literate individual.

They demonstrate independence.

Students can, without significant scaffolding, comprehend and evaluate complex texts across a range of types and disciplines, and they can construct effective arguments and convey intricate or multifaceted information. Likewise, students are independently able to discern a speaker's key points, request clarification, and ask relevant questions. They build on others' ideas, articulate their own ideas, and confirm they have been understood. Without prompting, they demonstrate command of standard English and acquire and use a wide-ranging vocabulary. More broadly, they become self-directed learners, effectively seeking out and using resources to assist them, including teachers, peers, and print and digital reference materials.

They build strong content knowledge.

Students establish a base of knowledge across a wide range of subject matter by engaging with works of quality and substance. They become proficient in new areas through research and study. They read purposefully and listen attentively to gain both general knowledge and discipline-specific expertise. They refine and share their knowledge through writing and speaking.

They respond to the varying demands of audience, task, purpose, and discipline.

Students adapt their communication in relation to audience, task, purpose, and discipline. They set and adjust purpose for reading, writing, speaking, listening, and language use as warranted by the task. They appreciate nuances, such as how the composition of an audience should affect tone when speaking and how the connotations of words affect meaning. They also know that different disciplines call for different types of evidence (e.g., documentary evidence in history, experimental evidence in science).

They comprehend as well as critique.

Students are engaged and open-minded—but discerning—readers and listeners. They work diligently to understand precisely what an author or speaker is saying, but they also question an author's or speaker's assumptions and premises and assess the veracity of claims and the soundness of reasoning.

They value evidence.

Students cite specific evidence when offering an oral or written interpretation of a text. They use relevant evidence when supporting their own points in writing and speaking, making their reasoning clear to the reader or listener, and they constructively evaluate others' use of evidence.

They use technology and digital media strategically and capably.

Students employ technology thoughtfully to enhance their reading, writing, speaking, listening, and language use. They tailor their searches online to acquire useful information efficiently, and they integrate what they learn through technology with what they learn offline. They are familiar with the strengths and limitations of various technological tools and media and can select and use those best suited to their communication goals.

They come to understand other perspectives and cultures.

Students appreciate that the twenty-first-century classroom and workplace are settings in which people from often widely divergent cultures and who represent diverse experiences and perspectives must learn and work together. Students actively seek to understand other perspectives and cultures through reading and listening, and they are able to communicate effectively with people of varied backgrounds. They evaluate other points of view critically and constructively. Through reading great classic and contemporary works of literature representative of a variety of periods, cultures, and worldviews, students can vicariously inhabit worlds and have experiences much different from their own.

How to Read This Document

Overall document organization

The Standards comprise three main sections, a comprehensive K–5 section and two content area-specific sections for grades 6–12: one for ELA and one for history/social studies, science, and technical subjects. Three appendices accompany the main document.

Each section is divided into strands. K–5 and grades 6–12 have Reading, Writing, Speaking and Listening, and Language strands; the grades 6–12 history/social studies, science, and technical subjects section focuses on Reading and Writing. Each strand is headed by a strand-specific set of College and Career Readiness anchor standards that is identical across all grades and content areas.

Standards for each grade within K–8 and for grades 9–10 and 11–12 follow the CCR anchor standards in each strand. Each grade-specific standard (as these standards are collectively referred to) corresponds to the same-numbered CCR anchor standard. Put another way, each CCR anchor standard has an accompanying grade-specific standard translating the broader CCR statement into grade-appropriate end-of-year expectations.

Individual CCR anchor standards can be identified by their strand, CCR status, and number (R.CCR.6, for example). Individual grade-specific standards can be identified by their strand, grade, and number (or number and letter, where applicable), so that RI.4.3, for example, stands for Reading, Informational Text, grade 4, standard 3, and W.5.1a stands for Writing, grade 5, standard 1a. Strand designations can be found in boxes before the full strand title. California additions to the standards are identified in boldface text followed by the abbreviation "CA."

Who is responsible for which portion of the Standards

A single K–5 section lists standards for reading, writing, speaking and listening, and language across the curriculum, reflecting the fact that most or all of the instruction students in these grades receive comes from one teacher. Grades 6–12 are covered in two content area–specific sections, the first for the English language arts teacher and the second for teachers of history/social studies, science, and technical subjects. Each section uses the same CCR anchor standards but also includes grade-specific standards tuned to the literacy requirements of the particular discipline(s).

Key Features of the Standards

Reading: Text complexity and the growth of comprehension

The Reading standards place equal emphasis on the sophistication of what students read and the skill with which they read. Standard 10 defines a grade-by-grade "staircase" of increasing text complexity that rises from beginning reading to the college and career readiness level. Whatever they are reading, students must also show a steadily growing ability to discern more from and make fuller use of text, including making an increasing number of connections among ideas and between texts, considering a wider range of textual evidence, and becoming more sensitive to inconsistencies, ambiguities, and poor reasoning in texts.

Writing: Text types, responding to reading, and research

The Standards acknowledge the fact that whereas some writing skills, such as the ability to plan, revise, edit, and publish, are applicable to many types of writing, other skills are more properly defined in terms of specific writing types: arguments, informative/explanatory texts, and narratives. Standard 9 stresses the importance of the writing-reading connection by requiring students to draw upon and write about evidence from literary and informational texts. Because of the centrality of writing to most forms of inquiry, research standards are prominently included in this strand, though skills important to research are infused throughout the document.

Speaking and Listening: Flexible communication and collaboration

Including but not limited to skills necessary for formal presentations, the Speaking and Listening standards require students to develop a range of broadly useful oral communication and interpersonal skills. Students must learn to work together, express and listen carefully to ideas, integrate information from oral, visual, quantitative, and media sources, evaluate what they hear, use media and visual displays strategically to help achieve communicative purposes, and adapt speech to context and task.

Language: Conventions, effective use, and vocabulary

The Language standards include the essential "rules" of standard written and spoken English. However, language is presented as a matter of craft and informed choice among alternatives. The vocabulary standards focus on understanding words and phrases, their relationships, and their nuances and on acquiring new vocabulary, particularly general academic and domain-specific words and phrases.

Appendices A, B, and C

Appendix A contains supplementary material on reading, writing, speaking and listening, and language as well as a glossary of key terms. Appendix B consists of text exemplars illustrating the complexity, quality, and range of reading appropriate for various grade levels with accompanying sample performance tasks. Appendix C includes annotated samples that demonstrate at least adequate performance in student writing at various grade levels.

The appendices are available on the Common Core State Standards Initiative Web site at http://www.corestandards.org/ELA-Literacy.

Standards for

English Language Arts & Literacy in History/Social Studies, Science, and Technical Subjects

K–5

College and Career Readiness Anchor Standards for Reading

The K–5 standards on the following pages define what students should understand and be able to do by the end of each grade. They correspond to the College and Career Readiness (CCR) anchor standards below by number. The CCR and grade-specific standards are necessary complements—the former providing broad standards, the latter providing additional specificity—that together define the skills and understandings that all students must demonstrate.

Key Ideas and Details

1. Read closely to determine what the text says explicitly and to make logical inferences from it; cite specific textual evidence when writing or speaking to support conclusions drawn from the text.

2. Determine central ideas or themes of a text and analyze their development; summarize the key supporting details and ideas.

3. Analyze how and why individuals, events, and ideas develop and interact over the course of a text.

Craft and Structure

4. Interpret words and phrases as they are used in a text, including determining technical, connotative, and figurative meanings, and analyze how specific word choices shape meaning or tone.

5. Analyze the structure of texts, including how specific sentences, paragraphs, and larger portions of the text (e.g., a section, chapter, scene, or stanza) relate to each other and the whole.

6. Assess how point of view or purpose shapes the content and style of a text.

Integration of Knowledge and Ideas

7. Integrate and evaluate content presented in diverse media and formats, including visually and quantitatively, as well as in words.*

8. Delineate and evaluate the argument and specific claims in a text, including the validity of the reasoning as well as the relevance and sufficiency of the evidence.[1]

9. Analyze how two or more texts address similar themes or topics in order to build knowledge or to compare the approaches the authors take.

Range of Reading and Level of Text Complexity

10. Read and comprehend complex literary and informational texts independently and proficiently.

Note on range and content of student reading

To build a foundation for college and career readiness, students must read widely and deeply from a broad range of high-quality, increasingly challenging literary and informational texts. Through extensive reading of stories, dramas, poems, and myths from diverse cultures and different time periods, students gain literary and cultural knowledge as well as familiarity with various text structures and elements. By reading texts in history/social studies, science, and other disciplines, students build a foundation of knowledge in those fields that will also give them the background to be better readers in all content areas. Students can gain this foundation only when the curriculum is intentionally and coherently structured to develop rich content knowledge within and across grades. Students also acquire the habits of reading independently and closely, which are essential to future success.

---

*Please see "Research to Build and Present Knowledge" in Writing and "Comprehension and Collaboration" in Speaking and Listening for additional standards relevant to gathering, assessing, and applying information from print and digital sources.

Reading Standards for Literature K–5

The following standards offer a focus for instruction each year and help ensure that students gain adequate exposure to a range of texts and tasks. Rigor is also infused through the requirement that students read increasingly complex texts through the grades. *Students advancing through the grades are expected to meet each year's grade-specific standards and retain or further develop skills and understandings mastered in preceding grades.*

	Kindergartners	Grade 1 Students	Grade 2 Students
Key Ideas and Details	1. With prompting and support, ask and answer questions about key details in a text.	1. Ask and answer questions about key details in a text.	1. Ask and answer such questions as *who, what, where, when, why,* and *how* to demonstrate understanding of key details in a text.
	2. With prompting and support, retell familiar stories, including key details.	2. Retell stories, including key details, and demonstrate understanding of their central message or lesson.	2. Recount stories, including fables and folktales from diverse cultures, and determine their central message, lesson, or moral.
	3. With prompting and support, identify characters, settings, and major events in a story.	3. Describe characters, settings, and major events in a story, using key details.	3. Describe how characters in a story respond to major events and challenges.
Craft and Structure	4. Ask and answer questions about unknown words in a text. **(See grade K Language standards 4–6 for additional expectations.) CA**	4. Identify words and phrases in stories or poems that suggest feelings or appeal to the senses. **(See grade 1 Language standards 4–6 for additional expectations.) CA**	4. Describe how words and phrases (e.g., regular beats, alliteration, rhymes, repeated lines) supply rhythm and meaning in a story, poem, or song. **(See grade 2 Language standards 4–6 for additional expectations.) CA**
	5. Recognize common types of texts (e.g., storybooks, poems, **fantasy, realistic text). CA**	5. Explain major differences between books that tell stories and books that give information, drawing on a wide reading of a range of text types.	5. Describe the overall structure of a story, including describing how the beginning introduces the story and the ending concludes the action.
	6. With prompting and support, name the author and illustrator of a story and define the role of each in telling the story.	6. Identify who is telling the story at various points in a text.	6. Acknowledge differences in the points of view of characters, including by speaking in a different voice for each character when reading dialogue aloud.
Integration of Knowledge and Ideas	7. With prompting and support, describe the relationship between illustrations and the story in which they appear (e.g., what moment in a story an illustration depicts).	7. Use illustrations and details in a story to describe its characters, setting, or events.	7. Use information gained from the illustrations and words in a print or digital text to demonstrate understanding of its characters, setting, or plot.
	8. (Not applicable to literature)	8. (Not applicable to literature)	8. (Not applicable to literature)
	9. With prompting and support, compare and contrast the adventures and experiences of characters in familiar stories.	9. Compare and contrast the adventures and experiences of characters in stories.	9. Compare and contrast two or more versions of the same story (e.g., Cinderella stories) by different authors or from different cultures.

	Kindergartners	Grade 1 Students	Grade 2 Students
Range of Reading and Level of Text Complexity	10. Actively engage in group reading activities with purpose and understanding. a. **Activate prior knowledge related to the information and events in texts. CA** b. **Use illustrations and context to make predictions about text. CA**	10. With prompting and support, read prose and poetry of appropriate complexity for grade 1. a. **Activate prior knowledge related to the information and events in a text. CA** b. **Confirm predictions about what will happen next in a text. CA**	10. By the end of the year, read and comprehend literature, including stories and poetry, in the grades 2–3 text complexity band proficiently, with scaffolding as needed at the high end of the range.

	Grade 3 Students	Grade 4 Students	Grade 5 Students
Key Ideas and Details	1. Ask and answer questions to demonstrate understanding of a text, referring explicitly to the text as the basis for the answers.	1. Refer to details and examples in a text when explaining what the text says explicitly and when drawing inferences from the text.	1. Quote accurately from a text when explaining what the text says explicitly and when drawing inferences from the text.
	2. Recount stories, including fables, folktales, and myths from diverse cultures; determine the central message, lesson, or moral and explain how it is conveyed through key details in the text.	2. Determine a theme of a story, drama, or poem from details in the text; summarize the text.	2. Determine a theme of a story, drama, or poem from details in the text, including how characters in a story or drama respond to challenges or how the speaker in a poem reflects upon a topic; summarize the text.
	3. Describe characters in a story (e.g., their traits, motivations, or feelings) and explain how their actions contribute to the sequence of events.	3. Describe in depth a character, setting, or event in a story or drama, drawing on specific details in the text (e.g., a character's thoughts, words, or actions).	3. Compare and contrast two or more characters, settings, or events in a story or drama, drawing on specific details in the text (e.g., how characters interact).

RL Reading Standards for Literature K–5

	Grade 3 Students	Grade 4 Students	Grade 5 Students
Craft and Structure	4. Determine the meaning of words and phrases as they are used in a text, distinguishing literal from nonliteral language. **(See grade 3 Language standards 4–6 for additional expectations.) CA**	4. Determine the meaning of words and phrases as they are used in a text, including those that allude to significant characters found in mythology (e.g., Herculean). **(See grade 4 Language standards 4–6 for additional expectations.) CA**	4. Determine the meaning of words and phrases as they are used in a text, including figurative language such as metaphors and similes. **(See grade 5 Language standards 4–6 for additional expectations.) CA**
	5. Refer to parts of stories, dramas, and poems when writing or speaking about a text, using terms such as chapter, scene, and stanza; describe how each successive part builds on earlier sections.	5. Explain major differences between poems, drama, and prose, and refer to the structural elements of poems (e.g., verse, rhythm, meter) and drama (e.g., casts of characters, settings, descriptions, dialogue, stage directions) when writing or speaking about a text.	5. Explain how a series of chapters, scenes, or stanzas fits together to provide the overall structure of a particular story, drama, or poem.
	6. Distinguish their own point of view from that of the narrator or those of the characters.	6. Compare and contrast the point of view from which different stories are narrated, including the difference between first- and third-person narrations.	6. Describe how a narrator's or speaker's point of view influences how events are described.
Integration of Knowledge and Ideas	7. Explain how specific aspects of a text's illustrations contribute to what is conveyed by the words in a story (e.g., create mood, emphasize aspects of a character or setting).	7. Make connections between the text of a story or drama and a visual or oral presentation of the text, identifying where each version reflects specific descriptions and directions in the text.	7. Analyze how visual and multimedia elements contribute to the meaning, tone, or beauty of a text (e.g., graphic novel, multimedia presentation of fiction, folktale, myth, poem).
	8. (Not applicable to literature)	8. (Not applicable to literature)	8. (Not applicable to literature)
	9. Compare and contrast the themes, settings, and plots of stories written by the same author about the same or similar characters (e.g., in books from a series).	9. Compare and contrast the treatment of similar themes and topics (e.g., opposition of good and evil) and patterns of events (e.g., the quest) in stories, myths, and traditional literature from different cultures.	9. Compare and contrast stories in the same genre (e.g., mysteries and adventure stories) on their approaches to similar themes and topics.
Range of Reading and Level of Text Complexity	10. By the end of the year, read and comprehend literature, including stories, dramas, and poetry, at the high end of the grades 2–3 text complexity band independently and proficiently.	10. By the end of the year, read and comprehend literature, including stories, dramas, and poetry, in the grades 4–5 text complexity band proficiently, with scaffolding as needed at the high end of the range.	10. By the end of the year, read and comprehend literature, including stories, dramas, and poetry, at the high end of the grades 4–5 text complexity band independently and proficiently.

RI

Reading Standards for Informational Text K–5

	Kindergartners	Grade 1 Students	Grade 2 Students
Key Ideas and Details	1. With prompting and support, ask and answer questions about key details in a text.	1. Ask and answer questions about key details in a text.	1. Ask and answer such questions as *who, what, where, when, why,* and *how* to demonstrate understanding of key details in a text.
	2. With prompting and support, identify the main topic and retell key details of a text.	2. Identify the main topic and retell key details of a text.	2. Identify the main topic of a multiparagraph text as well as the focus of specific paragraphs within the text.
	3. With prompting and support, describe the connection between two individuals, events, ideas, or pieces of information in a text.	3. Describe the connection between two individuals, events, ideas, or pieces of information in a text.	3. Describe the connection between a series of historical events, scientific ideas or concepts, or steps in technical procedures in a text.
Craft and Structure	4. With prompting and support, ask and answer questions about unknown words in a text. **(See grade K Language standards 4–6 additional expectations.) CA**	4. Ask and answer questions to help determine or clarify the meaning of words and phrases in a text. **(See grade 1 Language standards 4–6 for additional expectations.) CA**	4. Determine the meaning of words and phrases in a text relevant to a *grade 2 topic or subject area.* **(See grade 2 Language standards 4–6 for additional expectations.) CA**
	5. Identify the front cover, back cover, and title page of a book.	5. Know and use various text **structures (e.g., sequence) and text** features (e.g., headings, tables of contents, glossaries, electronic menus, icons) to locate key facts or information in a text. **CA**	5. Know and use various text features (e.g., captions, bold print, subheadings, glossaries, indexes, electronic menus, icons) to locate key facts or information in a text efficiently.
	6. Name the author and illustrator of a text and define the role of each in presenting the ideas or information in a text.	6. Distinguish between information provided by pictures or other illustrations and information provided by the words in a text.	6. Identify the main purpose of a text, including what the author wants to answer, explain, or describe.
Integration of Knowledge and Ideas	7. With prompting and support, describe the relationship between illustrations and the text in which they appear (e.g., what person, place, thing, or idea in the text an illustration depicts).	7. Use the illustrations and details in a text to describe its key ideas.	7. Explain how specific images (e.g., a diagram showing how a machine works) contribute to and clarify a text.
	8. With prompting and support, identify the reasons an author gives to support points in a text.	8. Identify the reasons an author gives to support points in a text.	8. Describe how reasons support specific points the author makes in a text.
	9. With prompting and support, identify basic similarities in and differences between two texts on the same topic (e.g., in illustrations, descriptions, or procedures).	9. Identify basic similarities in and differences between two texts on the same topic (e.g., in illustrations, descriptions, or procedures).	9. Compare and contrast the most important points presented by two texts on the same topic.

RI Reading Standards for Informational Text K–5

	Kindergartners	Grade 1 Students	Grade 2 Students

Range of Reading and Level of Text Complexity	10. Actively engage in group reading activities with purpose and understanding.
	
	  a. **Activate prior knowledge related to the information and events in texts. CA**
	
	  b. **Use illustrations and context to make predictions about text. CA**
		10. With prompting and support, read informational texts appropriately complex for grade 1.
		
		  a. **Activate prior knowledge related to the information and events in a text. CA**
		
		  b. **Confirm predictions about what will happen next in a text. CA**
			10. By the end of year, read and comprehend informational texts, including history/social studies, science, and technical texts, in the grades 2–3 text complexity band proficiently, with scaffolding as needed at the high end of the range.

	Grade 3 Students	Grade 4 Students	Grade 5 Students
Key Ideas and Details	1. Ask and answer questions to demonstrate understanding of a text, referring explicitly to the text as the basis for the answers.	1. Refer to details and examples in a text when explaining what the text says explicitly and when drawing inferences from the text.	1. Quote accurately from a text when explaining what the text says explicitly and when drawing inferences from the text.
	2. Determine the main idea of a text; recount the key details and explain how they support the main idea.	2. Determine the main idea of a text and explain how it is supported by key details; summarize the text.	2. Determine two or more main ideas of a text and explain how they are supported by key details; summarize the text.
	3. Describe the relationship between a series of historical events, scientific ideas or concepts, or steps in technical procedures in a text, using language that pertains to time, sequence, and cause/effect.	3. Explain events, procedures, ideas, or concepts in a historical, scientific, or technical text, including what happened and why, based on specific information in the text.	3. Explain the relationships or interactions between two or more individuals, events, ideas, or concepts in a historical, scientific, or technical text based on specific information in the text.
Craft and Structure	4. Determine the meaning of general academic and domain-specific words and phrases in a text relevant to a *grade 3 topic or subject area.* **(See grade 3 Language standards 4–6 for additional expectations.) CA**	4. Determine the meaning of general academic and domain-specific words or phrases in a text relevant to a *grade 4 topic or subject area.* **(See grade 4 Language standards 4–6 for additional expectations.) CA**	4. Determine the meaning of general academic and domain-specific words and phrases in a text relevant to a *grade 5 topic or subject area.* **(See grade 5 Language standards 4–6 for additional expectations.) CA**
	5. Use text features and search tools (e.g., key words, sidebars, hyperlinks) to locate information relevant to a given topic efficiently.	5. Describe the overall structure (e.g., chronology, comparison, cause/effect, problem/solution) of events, ideas, concepts, or information in a text or part of a text.	5. Compare and contrast the overall structure (e.g., chronology, comparison, cause/effect, problem/solution) of events, ideas, concepts, or information in two or more texts.
	6. Distinguish their own point of view from that of the author of a text.	6. Compare and contrast a firsthand and secondhand account of the same event or topic; describe the differences in focus and the information provided.	6. Analyze multiple accounts of the same event or topic, noting important similarities and differences in the point of view they represent.

RI Reading Standards for Informational Text K–5

	Grade 3 Students	Grade 4 Students	Grade 5 Students
Integration of Knowledge and Ideas	7. Use information gained from illustrations (e.g., maps, photographs) and the words in a text to demonstrate understanding of the text (e.g., where, when, why, and how key events occur).	7. Interpret information presented visually, orally, or quantitatively (e.g., in charts, graphs, diagrams, time lines, animations, or interactive elements on Web pages) and explain how the information contributes to an understanding of the text in which it appears.	7. Draw on information from multiple print or digital sources, demonstrating the ability to locate an answer to a question quickly or to solve a problem efficiently.
	8. Describe the logical connection between particular sentences and paragraphs in a text (e.g., comparison, cause/effect, first/second/third in a sequence).	8. Explain how an author uses reasons and evidence to support particular points in a text.	8. Explain how an author uses reasons and evidence to support particular points in a text, identifying which reasons and evidence support which point(s).
	9. Compare and contrast the most important points and key details presented in two texts on the same topic.	9. Integrate information from two texts on the same topic in order to write or speak about the subject knowledgeably.	9. Integrate information from several texts on the same topic in order to write or speak about the subject knowledgeably.
Range of Reading and Level of Text Complexity	10. By the end of the year, read and comprehend informational texts, including history/social studies, science, and technical texts, at the high end of the grades 2–3 text complexity band independently and proficiently.	10. By the end of year, read and comprehend informational texts, including history/social studies, science, and technical texts, in the grades 4–5 text complexity band proficiently, with scaffolding as needed at the high end of the range.	10. By the end of the year, read and comprehend informational texts, including history/social studies, science, and technical texts, at the high end of the grades 4–5 text complexity band independently and proficiently.

RF

Reading Standards for Foundational Skills K–5

These standards are directed toward fostering students' understanding and working knowledge of concepts of print, the alphabetic principle, and other basic conventions of the English writing system. These foundational skills are not an end in and of themselves; rather, they are necessary and important components of an effective, comprehensive reading program designed to develop proficient readers with the capacity to comprehend texts across a range of types and disciplines. Instruction should be differentiated: good readers will need much less practice with these concepts than struggling readers will. The point is to teach students what they need to learn and not what they already know—to discern when particular children or activities warrant more or less attention.

Note: In kindergarten, children are expected to demonstrate increasing awareness and competence in the areas that follow.

Kindergartners	Grade 1 Students

Print Concepts 1. Demonstrate understanding of the organization and basic features of print.
   a. Follow words from left to right, top to bottom, and page by page.
   b. Recognize that spoken words are represented in written language by specific sequences of letters.
   c. Understand that words are separated by spaces in print.
   d. Recognize and name all upper- and lowercase letters of the alphabet.
	1. Demonstrate understanding of the organization and basic features of print.
	   a. Recognize the distinguishing features of a sentence (e.g., first word, capitalization, ending punctuation).

Phonological Awareness 2. Demonstrate understanding of spoken words, syllables, and sounds (phonemes).
   a. Recognize and produce rhyming words.
   b. Count, pronounce, blend, and segment syllables in spoken words.
   c. Blend and segment onsets and rimes of single-syllable spoken words.
   d. Isolate and pronounce the initial, medial vowel, and final sounds (phonemes) in three-phoneme (consonant-vowel-consonant, or CVC) words.* (This does not include CVCs ending with /l/, /r/, or /x/.)
   e. Add or substitute individual sounds (phonemes) in simple, one-syllable words to make new words.
   f. Blend two to three phonemes into recognizable words. CA
	2. Demonstrate understanding of spoken words, syllables, and sounds (phonemes).
	   a. Distinguish long from short vowel sounds in spoken single-syllable words.
	   b. Orally produce single-syllable words by blending sounds (phonemes), including consonant blends.
	   c. Isolate and pronounce initial, medial vowel, and final sounds (phonemes) in spoken single-syllable words.
	   d. Segment spoken single-syllable words into their complete sequence of individual sounds (phonemes).

---

*Words, syllables, or phonemes written in /slashes/ refer to their pronunciation or phonology. Thus, /CVC/ is a word with three phonemes regardless of the number of letters in the spelling of the word.

RF | Reading Standards for Foundational Skills K–5

Note: In kindergarten, children are expected to demonstrate increasing awareness and competence in the areas that follow.

	Kindergartners	Grade 1 Students	Grade 2 Students
Phonics and Word Recognition	3. Know and apply grade-level phonics and word analysis skills in decoding words **both in isolation and in text. CA** a. Demonstrate basic knowledge of one-to-one letter-sound correspondences by producing the primary sounds or many of the most frequent sounds for each consonant. b. Associate the long and short sounds with common spellings (graphemes) for the five major vowels. **(Identify which letters represent the five major vowels [Aa, Ee, Ii, Oo, and Uu] and know the long and short sound of each vowel. More complex long vowel graphemes and spellings are targeted in the grade 1 phonics standards.) CA** c. Read common high-frequency words by sight (e.g., *the, of, to, you, she, my, is, are, do, does*). d. Distinguish between similarly spelled words by identifying the sounds of the letters that differ.	3. Know and apply grade-level phonics and word analysis skills in decoding words **both in isolation and in text. CA** a. Know the spelling-sound correspondences for common consonant digraphs. b. Decode regularly spelled one-syllable words. c. Know final -e and common vowel team conventions for representing long vowel sounds. d. Use knowledge that every syllable must have a vowel sound to determine the number of syllables in a printed word. e. Decode two-syllable words following basic patterns by breaking the words into syllables. f. Read words with inflectional endings. g. Recognize and read grade-appropriate irregularly spelled words.	3. Know and apply grade-level phonics and word analysis skills in decoding words **both in isolation and in text. CA** a. Distinguish long and short vowels when reading regularly spelled one-syllable words. b. Know spelling-sound correspondences for additional common vowel teams. c. Decode regularly spelled two-syllable words with long vowels. d. Decode words with common prefixes and suffixes. e. Identify words with inconsistent but common spelling-sound correspondences. f. Recognize and read grade-appropriate irregularly spelled words.
Fluency	4. Read emergent-reader texts with purpose and understanding.	4. Read with sufficient accuracy and fluency to support comprehension. a. Read on-level text with purpose and understanding. b. Read on-level text orally with accuracy, appropriate rate, and expression on successive readings. c. Use context to confirm or self-correct word recognition and understanding, rereading as necessary.	4. Read with sufficient accuracy and fluency to support comprehension. a. Read on-level text with purpose and understanding. b. Read on-level text orally with accuracy, appropriate rate, and expression on successive readings. c. Use context to confirm or self-correct word recognition and understanding, rereading as necessary.

	Grade 3 Students	Grade 4 Students	Grade 5 Students

Phonics and Word Recognition	3. Know and apply grade-level phonics and word analysis skills in decoding words **both in isolation and in text. CA**
	
	  a. Identify and know the meaning of the most common prefixes and derivational suffixes.
	
	  b. Decode words with common Latin suffixes.
	
	  c. Decode multisyllable words.
	
	  d. Read grade-appropriate irregularly spelled words.
		3. Know and apply grade-level phonics and word analysis skills in decoding words.
		
		  a. Use combined knowledge of all letter-sound correspondences, syllabication patterns, and morphology (e.g., roots and affixes) to read accurately unfamiliar multisyllabic words in context and out of context.
			3. Know and apply grade-level phonics and word analysis skills in decoding words.
			
			  a. Use combined knowledge of all letter-sound correspondences, syllabication patterns, and morphology (e.g., roots and affixes) to read accurately unfamiliar multisyllabic words in context and out of context.

Fluency	4. Read with sufficient accuracy and fluency to support comprehension.
	
	  a. Read on-level text with purpose and understanding.
	
	  b. Read on-level prose and poetry orally with accuracy, appropriate rate, and expression on successive readings
	
	  c. Use context to confirm or self-correct word recognition and understanding, rereading as necessary.
		4. Read with sufficient accuracy and fluency to support comprehension.
		
		  a. Read on-level text with purpose and understanding.
		
		  b. Read on-level prose and poetry orally with accuracy, appropriate rate, and expression on successive readings.
		
		  c. Use context to confirm or self-correct word recognition and understanding, rereading as necessary.
			4. Read with sufficient accuracy and fluency to support comprehension.
			
			  a. Read on-level text with purpose and understanding.
			
			  b. Read on-level prose and poetry orally with accuracy, appropriate rate, and expression on successive readings.
			
			  c. Use context to confirm or self-correct word recognition and understanding, rereading as necessary.

College and Career Readiness Anchor Standards for Writing

The K–5 standards on the following pages define what students should understand and be able to do by the end of each grade. They correspond to the College and Career Readiness (CCR) anchor standards below by number. The CCR and grade-specific standards are necessary complements—the former providing broad standards, the latter providing additional specificity—that together define the skills and understandings that all students must demonstrate.

Text Types and Purposes*

1. Write arguments to support claims in an analysis of substantive topics or texts, using valid reasoning and relevant and sufficient evidence.

2. Write informative/explanatory texts to examine and convey complex ideas and information clearly and accurately through the effective selection, organization, and analysis of content.

3. Write narratives to develop real or imagined experiences or events using effective technique, well-chosen details, and well-structured event sequences.

Production and Distribution of Writing

4. Produce clear and coherent writing in which the development, organization, and style are appropriate to task, purpose, and audience.

5. Develop and strengthen writing as needed by planning, revising, editing, rewriting, or trying a new approach.

6. Use technology, including the Internet, to produce and publish writing and to interact and collaborate with others.

*These broad types of writing include many subgenres. See Appendix A for definitions of key writing types.

Research to Build and Present Knowledge

7. Conduct short as well as more sustained research projects based on focused questions, demonstrating understanding of the subject under investigation.

8. Gather relevant information from multiple print and digital sources, assess the credibility and accuracy of each source, and integrate the information while avoiding plagiarism.

9. Draw evidence from literary and/or informational texts to support analysis, reflection, and research.

Range of Writing

10. Write routinely over extended time frames (time for research, reflection, and revision) and shorter time frames (a single sitting or a day or two) for a range of tasks, purposes, and audiences.

Note on range and content of student writing

To build a foundation for college and career readiness, students need to learn to use writing as a way of offering and supporting opinions, demonstrating understanding of the subjects they are studying, and conveying real and imagined experiences and events. They learn to appreciate that a key purpose of writing is to communicate clearly to an external, sometimes unfamiliar audience, and they begin to adapt the form and content of their writing to accomplish a particular task and purpose. They develop the capacity to build knowledge on a subject through research projects and to respond analytically to literary and informational sources. To meet these goals, students must devote significant time and effort to writing, producing numerous pieces over short and extended time frames throughout the year.

Writing Standards K–5

The following standards for K–5 offer a focus for instruction each year to help ensure that students gain adequate mastery of a range of skills and applications. Each year in their writing, students should demonstrate increasing sophistication in all aspects of language use, from vocabulary and syntax to the development and organization of ideas, and they should address increasingly demanding content and sources. *Students advancing through the grades are expected to meet each year's grade-specific standards and retain or further develop skills and understandings mastered in preceding grades.* The expected growth in student writing ability is reflected both in the standards themselves and in the collection of annotated student writing samples in Appendix C.

	Kindergartners	Grade 1 Students	Grade 2 Students
Text Types and Purposes	1. Use a combination of drawing, dictating, and writing to compose opinion pieces in which they tell a reader the topic or the name of the book they are writing about and state an opinion or preference about the topic or book (e.g., *My favorite book is . . .*).	1. Write opinion pieces in which they introduce the topic or name the book they are writing about, state an opinion, supply a reason for the opinion, and provide some sense of closure.	1. Write opinion pieces in which they introduce the topic or book they are writing about, state an opinion, supply reasons that support the opinion, use linking words (e.g., *because, and, also*) to connect opinion and reasons, and provide a concluding statement or section.
	2. Use a combination of drawing, dictating, and writing to compose informative/explanatory texts in which they name what they are writing about and supply some information about the topic.	2. Write informative/explanatory texts in which they name a topic, supply some facts about the topic, and provide some sense of closure.	2. Write informative/explanatory texts in which they introduce a topic, use facts and definitions to develop points, and provide a concluding statement or section.
	3. Use a combination of drawing, dictating, and writing to narrate a single event or several loosely linked events, tell about the events in the order in which they occurred, and provide a reaction to what happened.	3. Write narratives in which they recount two or more appropriately sequenced events, include some details regarding what happened, use temporal words to signal event order, and provide some sense of closure.	3. Write narratives in which they recount a well-elaborated event or short sequence of events, include details to describe actions, thoughts, and feelings, use temporal words to signal event order, and provide a sense of closure.
Production and Distribution of Writing	4. (Begins in grade **2**) **CA**	4. (Begins in grade **2**) **CA**	4. **With guidance and support from adults, produce writing in which the development and organization are appropriate to task and purpose. (Grade-specific expectations for writing types are defined in standards 1–3 above.) CA**
	5. With guidance and support from adults, respond to questions and suggestions from peers and add details to strengthen writing as needed.	5. With guidance and support from adults, focus on a topic, respond to questions and suggestions from peers, and add details to strengthen writing as needed.	5. With guidance and support from adults and peers, focus on a topic and strengthen writing as needed by revising and editing.
	6. With guidance and support from adults, explore a variety of digital tools to produce and publish writing, including in collaboration with peers.	6. With guidance and support from adults, use a variety of digital tools to produce and publish writing, including in collaboration with peers.	6. With guidance and support from adults, use a variety of digital tools to produce and publish writing, including in collaboration with peers.

	Kindergartners	Grade 1 Students	Grade 2 Students
Research to Build and Present Knowledge	7. Participate in shared research and writing projects (e.g., explore a number of books by a favorite author and express opinions about them).	7. Participate in shared research and writing projects (e.g., explore a number of "how-to" books on a given topic and use them to write a sequence of instructions).	7. Participate in shared research and writing projects (e.g., read a number of books on a single topic to produce a report; record science observations).
	8. With guidance and support from adults, recall information from experiences or gather information from provided sources to answer a question.	8. With guidance and support from adults, recall information from experiences or gather information from provided sources to answer a question.	8. Recall information from experiences or gather information from provided sources to answer a question.
	9. (Begins in grade 4)	9. (Begins in grade 4)	9. (Begins in grade 4)
Range of Writing	10. (Begins in grade **2**) **CA**	10. (Begins in grade **2**) **CA**	10. **Write routinely over extended time frames (time for research, reflection, and revision) and shorter time frames (a single sitting or a day or two) for a range of discipline-specific tasks, purposes, and audiences. CA**

	Grade 3 Students	Grade 4 Students	Grade 5 Students
Text Types and Purposes	1. Write opinion pieces on topics or texts, supporting a point of view with reasons. a. Introduce the topic or text they are writing about, state an opinion, and create an organizational structure that lists reasons. b. Provide reasons that support the opinion. c. Use linking words and phrases (e.g., *because, therefore, since, for example*) to connect opinion and reasons. d. Provide a concluding statement or section.	1. Write opinion pieces on topics or texts, supporting a point of view with reasons and information. a. Introduce a topic or text clearly, state an opinion, and create an organizational structure in which related ideas are grouped to support the writer's purpose. b. Provide reasons that are supported by facts and details. c. Link opinion and reasons using words and phrases (e.g., *for instance, in order to, in addition*). d. Provide a concluding statement or section related to the opinion presented.	1. Write opinion pieces on topics or texts, supporting a point of view with reasons and information. a. Introduce a topic or text clearly, state an opinion, and create an organizational structure in which ideas are logically grouped to support the writer's purpose. b. Provide logically ordered reasons that are supported by facts and details. c. Link opinion and reasons using words, phrases, and clauses (e.g., *consequently, specifically*). d. Provide a concluding statement or section related to the opinion presented.

	Grade 3 Students	Grade 4 Students	Grade 5 Students
Text Types and Purposes *(continued)*	2. Write informative/explanatory texts to examine a topic and convey ideas and information clearly. a. Introduce a topic and group related information together; include illustrations when useful to aiding comprehension. b. Develop the topic with facts, definitions, and details. c. Use linking words and phrases (e.g., *also, another, and, more, but*) to connect ideas within categories of information. d. Provide a concluding statement or section.	2. Write informative/explanatory texts to examine a topic and convey ideas and information clearly. a. Introduce a topic clearly and group related information in paragraphs and sections; include formatting (e.g., headings), illustrations, and multimedia when useful to aiding comprehension. b. Develop the topic with facts, definitions, concrete details, quotations, or other information and examples related to the topic. c. Link ideas within categories of information using words and phrases (e.g., *another, for example, also, because*). d. Use precise language and domain-specific vocabulary to inform about or explain the topic. e. Provide a concluding statement or section related to the information or explanation presented.	2. Write informative/explanatory texts to examine a topic and convey ideas and information clearly. a. Introduce a topic clearly, provide a general observation and focus, and group related information logically; include formatting (e.g., headings), illustrations, and multimedia when useful to aiding comprehension. b. Develop the topic with facts, definitions, concrete details, quotations, or other information and examples related to the topic. c. Link ideas within and across categories of information using words, phrases, and clauses (e.g., *in contrast, especially*). d. Use precise language and domain-specific vocabulary to inform about or explain the topic. e. Provide a concluding statement or section related to the information or explanation presented.
	3. Write narratives to develop real or imagined experiences or events using effective technique, descriptive details, and clear event sequences. a. Establish a situation and introduce a narrator and/or characters; organize an event sequence that unfolds naturally. b. Use dialogue and descriptions of actions, thoughts, and feelings to develop experiences and events or show the response of characters to situations. c. Use temporal words and phrases to signal event order. d. Provide a sense of closure.	3. Write narratives to develop real or imagined experiences or events using effective technique, descriptive details, and clear event sequences. a. Orient the reader by establishing a situation and introducing a narrator and/or characters; organize an event sequence that unfolds naturally. b. Use dialogue and description to develop experiences and events or show the responses of characters to situations. c. Use a variety of transitional words and phrases to manage the sequence of events. d. Use concrete words and phrases and sensory details to convey experiences and events precisely. e. Provide a conclusion that follows from the narrated experiences or events.	3. Write narratives to develop real or imagined experiences or events using effective technique, descriptive details, and clear event sequences. a. Orient the reader by establishing a situation and introducing a narrator and/or characters; organize an event sequence that unfolds naturally. b. Use narrative techniques, such as dialogue, description, and pacing, to develop experiences and events or show the responses of characters to situations. c. Use a variety of transitional words, phrases, and clauses to manage the sequence of events. d. Use concrete words and phrases and sensory details to convey experiences and events precisely. e. Provide a conclusion that follows from the narrated experiences or events.

W Writing Standards K–5

	Grade 3 Students	Grade 4 Students	Grade 5 Students
Production and Distribution of Writing	4. With guidance and support from adults, produce writing in which the development and organization are appropriate to task and purpose. (Grade-specific expectations for writing types are defined in standards 1–3 above.)	4. Produce clear and coherent writing **(including multiple-paragraph texts)** in which the development and organization are appropriate to task, purpose, and audience. (Grade-specific expectations for writing types are defined in standards 1–3 above.) **CA**	4. Produce clear and coherent writing **(including multiple-paragraph texts)** in which the development and organization are appropriate to task, purpose, and audience. (Grade-specific expectations for writing types are defined in standards 1–3 above.) **CA**
	5. With guidance and support from peers and adults, develop and strengthen writing as needed by planning, revising, and editing. (Editing for conventions should demonstrate command of Language standards 1–3 up to and including grade 3.)	5. With guidance and support from peers and adults, develop and strengthen writing as needed by planning, revising, and editing. (Editing for conventions should demonstrate command of Language standards 1–3 up to and including grade 4.)	5. With guidance and support from peers and adults, develop and strengthen writing as needed by planning, revising, editing, rewriting, or trying a new approach. (Editing for conventions should demonstrate command of Language standards 1–3 up to and including grade 5.)
	6. With guidance and support from adults, use technology to produce and publish writing (using keyboarding skills) as well as to interact and collaborate with others.	6. With some guidance and support from adults, use technology, including the Internet, to produce and publish writing as well as to interact and collaborate with others; demonstrate sufficient command of keyboarding skills to type a minimum of one page in a single sitting.	6 With some guidance and support from adults, use technology, including the Internet, to produce and publish writing as well as to interact and collaborate with others; demonstrate sufficient command of keyboarding skills to type a minimum of two pages in a single sitting.
Research to Build and Present Knowledge	7. Conduct short research projects that build knowledge about a topic.	7. Conduct short research projects that build knowledge through investigation of different aspects of a topic.	7. Conduct short research projects that use several sources to build knowledge through investigation of different aspects of a topic.
	8. Recall information from experiences or gather information from print and digital sources; take brief notes on sources and sort evidence into provided categories.	8. Recall relevant information from experiences or gather relevant information from print and digital sources; take notes, **paraphrase,** and categorize information, and provide a list of sources. **CA**	8. Recall relevant information from experiences or gather relevant information from print and digital sources; summarize or paraphrase information in notes and finished work, and provide a list of sources.

W Writing Standards K–5

	Grade 3 Students	Grade 4 Students	Grade 5 Students
Research to Build and Present Knowledge (continued)	9. (Begins in grade 4)	9. Draw evidence from literary or informational texts to support analysis, reflection, and research. a. Apply *grade 4 Reading standards* to literature (e.g., "Describe in depth a character, setting, or event in a story or drama, drawing on specific details in the text [e.g., a character's thoughts, words, or actions]."). b. Apply *grade 4 Reading standards* to informational texts (e.g., "Explain how an author uses reasons and evidence to support particular points in a text").	9. Draw evidence from literary or informational texts to support analysis, reflection, and research. a. Apply *grade 5 Reading standards* to literature (e.g., "Compare and contrast two or more characters, settings, or events in a story or a drama, drawing on specific details in the text [e.g., how characters interact]"). b. Apply *grade 5 Reading standards* to informational texts (e.g., "Explain how an author uses reasons and evidence to support particular points in a text, identifying which reasons and evidence support which point[s]").
Range of Writing	10. Write routinely over extended time frames (time for research, reflection, and revision) and shorter time frames (a single sitting or a day or two) for a range of discipline-specific tasks, purposes, and audiences.	10. Write routinely over extended time frames (time for research, reflection, and revision) and shorter time frames (a single sitting or a day or two) for a range of discipline-specific tasks, purposes, and audiences.	10. Write routinely over extended time frames (time for research, reflection, and revision) and shorter time frames (a single sitting or a day or two) for a range of discipline-specific tasks, purposes, and audiences.

College and Career Readiness Anchor Standards for Speaking and Listening

The K–5 standards on the following pages define what students should understand and be able to do by the end of each grade. They correspond to the College and Career Readiness (CCR) anchor standards below by number. The CCR and grade-specific standards are necessary complements—the former providing broad standards, the latter providing additional specificity—that together define the skills and understandings that all students must demonstrate.

Comprehension and Collaboration

1. Prepare for and participate effectively in a range of conversations and collaborations with diverse partners, building on others' ideas and expressing their own clearly and persuasively.

2. Integrate and evaluate information presented in diverse media and formats, including visually, quantitatively, and orally.

3. Evaluate a speaker's point of view, reasoning, and use of evidence and rhetoric.

Presentation of Knowledge and Ideas

4. Present information, findings, and supporting evidence such that listeners can follow the line of reasoning and the organization, development, and style are appropriate to task, purpose, and audience.

5. Make strategic use of digital media and visual displays of data to express information and enhance understanding of presentations.

6. Adapt speech to a variety of contexts and communicative tasks, demonstrating command of formal English when indicated or appropriate.

Note on range and content of student speaking and listening

To build a foundation for college and career readiness, students must have ample opportunities to take part in a variety of rich, structured conversations—as part of a whole class, in small groups, and with a partner. Being productive members of these conversations requires that students contribute accurate, relevant information; respond to and develop what others have said; make comparisons and contrasts; and analyze and synthesize a multitude of ideas in various domains.

New technologies have broadened and expanded the role that speaking and listening play in acquiring and sharing knowledge and have tightened their link to other forms of communication. Digital texts confront students with the potential for continually updated content and dynamically changing combinations of words, graphics, images, hyperlinks, and embedded video and audio.

Speaking and Listening Standards K–5

The following standards for K–5 offer a focus for instruction each year to help ensure that students gain adequate mastery of a range of skills and applications. *Students advancing through the grades are expected to meet each year's grade-specific standards and retain or further develop skills and understandings mastered in preceding grades.*

	Kindergartners	Grade 1 Students	Grade 2 Students
Comprehension and Collaboration	1. Participate in collaborative conversations with diverse partners *about kindergarten topics and texts* with peers and adults in small and larger groups. a. Follow agreed-upon rules for discussions (e.g., listening to others and taking turns speaking about the topics and texts under discussion). b. Continue a conversation through multiple exchanges.	1. Participate in collaborative conversations with diverse partners about *grade 1 topics and texts* with peers and adults in small and larger groups. a. Follow agreed-upon rules for discussions (e.g., listening to others with care, speaking one at a time about the topics and texts under discussion). b. Build on others' talk in conversations by responding to the comments of others through multiple exchanges. c. Ask questions to clear up any confusion about the topics and texts under discussion.	1. Participate in collaborative conversations with diverse partners about *grade 2 topics and texts* with peers and adults in small and larger groups. a. Follow agreed-upon rules for discussions (e.g., gaining the floor in respectful ways listening to others with care, speaking one at a time about the topics and texts under discussion). b. Build on others' talk in conversations by linking their comments to the remarks of others. c. Ask for clarification and further explanation as needed about the topics and texts under discussion.
	2. Confirm understanding of a text read aloud or information presented orally or through other media by asking and answering questions about key details and requesting clarification if something is not understood. a. **Understand and follow one- and two-step oral directions. CA**	2. Ask and answer questions about key details in a text read aloud or information presented orally or through other media. a. **Give, restate, and follow simple two-step directions. CA**	2. Recount or describe key ideas or details from a text read aloud or information presented orally or through other media. a. **Give and follow three- and four-step oral directions. CA**
	3. Ask and answer questions in order to seek help, get information, or clarify something that is not understood.	3. Ask and answer questions about what a speaker says in order to gather additional information or clarify something that is not understood.	3. Ask and answer questions about what a speaker says in order to clarify comprehension, gather additional information, or deepen understanding of a topic or issue.

	Kindergartners	Grade 1 Students	Grade 2 Students
Presentation of Knowledge and Ideas	4. Describe familiar people, places, things, and events and, with prompting and support, provide additional detail.	4. Describe people, places, things, and events with relevant details, expressing ideas and feelings clearly. a. Memorize and recite poems, rhymes, and songs with expression. CA	4. Tell a story or recount an experience with appropriate facts and relevant, descriptive details, speaking audibly in coherent sentences. a. Plan and deliver a narrative presentation that: recounts a well-elaborated event, includes details, reflects a logical sequence, and provides a conclusion. CA
	5. Add drawings or other visual displays to descriptions as desired to provide additional detail.	5. Add drawings or other visual displays to descriptions when appropriate to clarify ideas, thoughts, and feelings.	5. Create audio recordings of stories or poems; add drawings or other visual displays to stories or recounts of experiences when appropriate to clarify ideas, thoughts, and feelings.
	6. Speak audibly and express thoughts, feelings, and ideas clearly.	6. Produce complete sentences when appropriate to task and situation. (See grade 1 Language standards 1 and 3 for specific expectations.)	6. Produce complete sentences when appropriate to task and situation in order to provide requested detail or clarification. (See grade 2 Language standards 1 and 3 for specific expectations.)

Grade 3 Students	Grade 4 Students	Grade 5 Students

Comprehension and Collaboration
 	
1. Engage effectively in a range of collaborative discussions (one-on-one, in groups, and teacher-led) with diverse partners on *grade 3 topics and texts,* building on others' ideas and expressing their own clearly.
 	
  a. Come to discussions prepared, having read or studied required material; explicitly draw on that preparation and other information known about the topic to explore ideas under discussion.
 	
  b. Follow agreed-upon rules for discussions (e.g., gaining the floor in respectful ways, listening to others with care, speaking one at a time about the topics and texts under discussion).
 	
  c. Ask questions to check understanding of information presented, stay on topic, and link their comments to the remarks of others.
 	
  d. Explain their own ideas and understanding in light of the discussion.
	1. Engage effectively in a range of collaborative discussions (one-on-one, in groups, and teacher-led) with diverse partners on *grade 4 topics and texts,* building on others' ideas and expressing their own clearly.
	
	  a. Come to discussions prepared, having read or studied required material; explicitly draw on that preparation and other information known about the topic to explore ideas under discussion.
	
	  b. Follow agreed-upon rules for discussions and carry out assigned roles.
	
	  c. Pose and respond to specific questions to clarify or follow up on information, and make comments that contribute to the discussion and link to the remarks of others.
	
	  d. Review the key ideas expressed and explain their own ideas and understanding in light of the discussion.
		1. Engage effectively in a range of collaborative discussions (one-on-one, in groups, and teacher-led) with diverse partners on *grade 5 topics and texts,* building on others' ideas and expressing their own clearly.
		
		  a. Come to discussions prepared, having read or studied required material; explicitly draw on that preparation and other information known about the topic to explore ideas under discussion.
		
		  b. Follow agreed-upon rules for discussions and carry out assigned roles.
		
		  c. Pose and respond to specific questions by making comments that contribute to the discussion and elaborate on the remarks of others.
		
		  d. Review the key ideas expressed and draw conclusions in light of information and knowledge gained from the discussions.

2. Determine the main ideas and supporting details of a text read aloud or information presented in diverse media and formats, including visually, quantitatively, and orally.	2. Paraphrase portions of a text read aloud or information presented in diverse media and formats, including visually, quantitatively, and orally.	2. Summarize a written text read aloud or information presented in diverse media and formats, including visually, quantitatively, and orally.
3. Ask and answer questions about information from a speaker, offering appropriate elaboration and detail.	3. Identify the reasons and evidence a speaker **or media source** provides to support particular points. **CA**	3. Summarize the points a speaker **or media source** makes and explain how each claim is supported by reasons and evidence, **and identify and analyze any logical fallacies. CA**

	Grade 3 Students	Grade 4 Students	Grade 5 Students

Presentation of Knowledge and Ideas	4. Report on a topic or text, tell a story, or recount an experience with appropriate facts and relevant, descriptive details, speaking clearly at an understandable pace.
	
	  a. **Plan and deliver an informative/explanatory presentation on a topic that: organizes ideas around major points of information, follows a logical sequence, includes supporting details, uses clear and specific vocabulary, and provides a strong conclusion. CA**
		4. Report on a topic or text, tell a story, or recount an experience in an organized manner, using appropriate facts and relevant, descriptive details to support main ideas or themes; speak clearly at an understandable pace.
		
		  a. **Plan and deliver a narrative presentation that: relates ideas, observations, or recollections; provides a clear context; and includes clear insight into why the event or experience is memorable. CA**
			4. Report on a topic or text or present an opinion, sequencing ideas logically and using appropriate facts and relevant, descriptive details to support main ideas or themes; speak clearly at an understandable pace.
			
			  a. **Plan and deliver an opinion speech that: states an opinion, logically sequences evidence to support the speaker's position, uses transition words to effectively link opinions and evidence (e.g., consequently and therefore), and provides a concluding statement related to the speaker's position. CA**
			
			  b. **Memorize and recite a poem or section of a speech or historical document using rate, expression, and gestures appropriate to the selection. CA**

	5. Create engaging audio recordings of stories or poems that demonstrate fluid reading at an understandable pace; add visual displays when appropriate to emphasize or enhance certain facts or details.	5. Add audio recordings and visual displays to presentations when appropriate to enhance the development of main ideas or themes.	5. Include multimedia components (e.g., graphics, sound) and visual displays in presentations when appropriate to enhance the development of main ideas or themes.
	6. Speak in complete sentences when appropriate to task and situation in order to provide requested detail or clarification. (See grade 3 Language standards 1 and 3 for specific expectations.)	6. Differentiate between contexts that call for formal English (e.g., presenting ideas) and situations where informal discourse is appropriate (e.g., small-group discussion); use formal English when appropriate to task and situation. (See grade 4 Language standards 1 and 3 for specific expectations.)	6. Adapt speech to a variety of contexts and tasks, using formal English when appropriate to task and situation. (See grade 5 Language standards 1 and 3 for specific expectations.)

College and Career Readiness Anchor Standards for Language

The K–5 standards on the following pages define what students should understand and be able to do by the end of each grade. They correspond to the College and Career Readiness (CCR) anchor standards below by number. The CCR and grade-specific standards are necessary complements—the former providing broad standards, the latter providing additional specificity—that together define the skills and understandings that all students must demonstrate.

Conventions of Standard English

1. Demonstrate command of the conventions of standard English grammar and usage when writing or speaking.

2. Demonstrate command of the conventions of standard English capitalization, punctuation, and spelling when writing.

Knowledge of Language

3. Apply knowledge of language to understand how language functions in different contexts, to make effective choices for meaning or style, and to comprehend more fully when reading or listening.

Vocabulary Acquisition and Use

4. Determine or clarify the meaning of unknown and multiple-meaning words and phrases by using context clues, analyzing meaningful word parts, and consulting general and specialized reference materials, as appropriate.

5. Demonstrate understanding of figurative language, word relationships, and nuances in word meanings.

6. Acquire and use accurately a range of general academic and domain-specific words and phrases sufficient for reading, writing, speaking, and listening at the college- and career-readiness level; demonstrate independence in gathering vocabulary knowledge when encountering an unknown term important to comprehension or expression.

> **Note on range and content of student language use**
>
> *To build a foundation for college and career readiness in language, students must gain control over many conventions of standard English grammar, usage, and mechanics as well as learn other ways to use language to convey meaning effectively. They must also be able to determine or clarify the meaning of grade-appropriate words encountered through listening, reading, and media use; come to appreciate that words have nonliteral meanings, shades of meaning, and relationships to other words; and expand their vocabulary in the course of studying content. The inclusion of Language standards in their own strand should not be taken as an indication that skills related to conventions, effective language use, and vocabulary are unimportant to reading, writing, speaking, and listening; indeed, they are inseparable from such contexts.*

Language Standards K–5

The following standards for grades K–5 offer a focus for instruction each year to help ensure that students gain adequate mastery of a range of skills and applications. *Students advancing through the grades are expected to meet each year's grade-specific standards and retain or further develop skills and understandings mastered in preceding grades.* Beginning in grade 3, skills and understandings that are particularly likely to require continued attention in higher grades as they are applied to increasingly sophisticated writing and speaking are marked with an asterisk (*). See the table "Language Progressive Skills, by Grade" on page 40 for a complete list and Appendix A for an example of how those skills develop in sophistication.

	Kindergartners	Grade 1 Students	Grade 2 Students
Conventions of Standard English	1. Demonstrate command of the conventions of standard English grammar and usage when writing or speaking. a. Print many upper- and lowercase letters. b. Use frequently occurring nouns and verbs. c. Form regular plural nouns orally by adding /s/ or /es/ (e.g., *dog, dogs; wish, wishes*). d. Understand and use question words (interrogatives) (e.g., *who, what, where, when, why, how*). e. Use the most frequently occurring prepositions (e.g., *to, from, in, out, on, off, for, of, by, with*). f. Produce and expand complete sentences in shared language activities.	1. Demonstrate command of the conventions of standard English grammar and usage when writing or speaking. a. Print all upper- and lowercase letters. b. Use common, proper, and possessive nouns. c. Use singular and plural nouns with matching verbs in basic sentences (e.g., *He hops; We hop*). d. Use personal **(subject, object)**, possessive, and indefinite pronouns (e.g., *I, me, my; they, them, their; anyone, everything*). **CA** e. Use verbs to convey a sense of past, present, and future (e.g., *Yesterday I walked home; Today I walk home; Tomorrow I will walk home*). f. Use frequently occurring adjectives. g. Use frequently occurring conjunctions (e.g., *and, but, or, so, because*). h. Use determiners (e.g., articles, demonstratives). i. Use frequently occurring prepositions (e.g., *during, beyond, toward*). j. Produce and expand complete simple and compound declarative, interrogative, imperative, and exclamatory sentences in response to prompts.	1. Demonstrate command of the conventions of standard English grammar and usage when writing or speaking. a. Use collective nouns (e.g., *group*). b. Form and use frequently occurring irregular plural nouns (e.g., *feet, children, teeth, mice, fish*). c. Use reflexive pronouns (e.g., *myself, ourselves*). d. Form and use the past tense of frequently occurring irregular verbs (e.g., *sat, hid, told*). e. Use adjectives and adverbs, and choose between them depending on what is to be modified. f. Produce, expand, and rearrange complete simple and compound sentences (e.g., *The boy watched the movie; The little boy watched the movie; The action movie was watched by the little boy*). g. **Create readable documents with legible print. CA**

	Kindergartners	Grade 1 Students	Grade 2 Students
Conventions of Standard English *(continued)*	2. Demonstrate command of the conventions of standard English capitalization, punctuation, and spelling when writing. a. Capitalize the first word in a sentence and the pronoun *I*. b. Recognize and name end punctuation. c. Write a letter or letters for most consonant and short-vowel sounds (phonemes). d. Spell simple words phonetically, drawing on knowledge of sound-letter relationships.	2. Demonstrate command of the conventions of standard English capitalization, punctuation, and spelling when writing. a. Capitalize dates and names of people. b. Use end punctuation for sentences. c. Use commas in dates and to separate single words in a series. d. Use conventional spelling for words with common spelling patterns and for frequently occurring irregular words. e. Spell untaught words phonetically, drawing on phonemic awareness and spelling conventions.	2. Demonstrate command of the conventions of standard English capitalization, punctuation, and spelling when writing. a. Capitalize holidays, product names, and geographic names. b. Use commas in greetings and closings of letters. c. Use an apostrophe to form contractions and frequently occurring possessives. d. Generalize learned spelling patterns when writing words (e.g., cage → badge; boy → boil). e. Consult reference materials, including beginning dictionaries, as needed to check and correct spellings.
Knowledge of Language	3. (Begins in grade 2)	3. (Begins in grade 2)	3. Use knowledge of language and its conventions when writing, speaking, reading, or listening. a. Compare formal and informal uses of English.

	Kindergartners	Grade 1 Students	Grade 2 Students

Vocabulary Acquisition and Use	4. Determine or clarify the meaning of unknown and multiple-meaning words and phrases based on *kindergarten reading and content.*
	
	  a. Identify new meanings for familiar words and apply them accurately (e.g., knowing *duck* is a bird and learning the verb *to duck*).
	
	  b. Use the most frequently occurring inflections and affixes (e.g., *-ed, -s, re-, un-, pre-, -ful, -less*) as a clue to the meaning of an unknown word.
		4. Determine or clarify the meaning of unknown and multiple-meaning words and phrases based on *grade 1 reading and content,* choosing flexibly from an array of strategies.
		
		  a. Use sentence-level context as a clue to the meaning of a word or phrase.
		
		  b. Use frequently occurring affixes as a clue to the meaning of a word.
		
		  c. Identify frequently occurring root words (e.g., *look*) and their inflectional forms (e.g., *looks, looked, looking*).
			4. Determine or clarify the meaning of unknown and multiple-meaning words and phrases based on *grade 2 reading and content,* choosing flexibly from an array of strategies.
			
			  a. Use sentence-level context as a clue to the meaning of a word or phrase.
			
			  b. Determine the meaning of the new word formed when a known prefix is added to a known word (e.g., *happy/unhappy, tell/retell*).
			
			  c. Use a known root word as a clue to the meaning of an unknown word with the same root (e.g., *addition, additional*).
			
			  d. Use knowledge of the meaning of individual words to predict the meaning of compound words (e.g., *birdhouse, lighthouse, housefly; bookshelf, notebook, bookmark*).
			
			  e. Use glossaries and beginning dictionaries, both print and digital, to determine or clarify the meaning of words and phrases **in all content areas. CA**

	Kindergartners	Grade 1 Students	Grade 2 Students
Vocabulary Acquisition and Use *(continued)*	5. With guidance and support from adults, explore word relationships and nuances in word meanings. a. Sort common objects into categories (e.g., shapes, foods) to gain a sense of the concepts the categories represent. b. Demonstrate understanding of frequently occurring verbs and adjectives by relating them to their opposites (antonyms). c. Identify real-life connections between words and their use (e.g., note places at school that are *colorful*). d. Distinguish shades of meaning among verbs describing the same general action (e.g., *walk, march, strut, prance*) by acting out the meanings.	5. With guidance and support from adults, demonstrate understanding of word relationships and nuances in word meanings. a. Sort words into categories (e.g., colors, clothing) to gain a sense of the concepts the categories represent. b. Define words by category and by one or more key attributes (e.g., a *duck* is a bird that swims; a *tiger* is a large cat with stripes). c. Identify real-life connections between words and their use (e.g., note places at home that are *cozy*). d. Distinguish shades of meaning among verbs differing in manner (e.g., *look, peek, glance, stare, glare, scowl*) and adjectives differing in intensity (e.g., *large, gigantic*) by defining or choosing them or by acting out the meanings.	5. Demonstrate understanding of word relationships and nuances in word meanings. a. Identify real-life connections between words and their use (e.g., describe foods that are *spicy* or *juicy*). b. Distinguish shades of meaning among closely related verbs (e.g., *toss, throw, hurl*) and closely related adjectives (e.g., *thin, slender, skinny, scrawny*).
	6. Use words and phrases acquired through conversations, reading and being read to, and responding to texts.	6. Use words and phrases acquired through conversations, reading and being read to, and responding to texts, including using frequently occurring conjunctions to signal simple relationships (e.g., *because*).	6. Use words and phrases acquired through conversations, reading and being read to, and responding to texts, including using adjectives and adverbs to describe (e.g., *When other kids are happy that makes me happy*).

L Language Standards K–5

	Grade 3 Students	Grade 4 Students	Grade 5 Students
Conventions of Standard English	1. Demonstrate command of the conventions of standard English grammar and usage when writing or speaking. a. Explain the function of nouns, pronouns, verbs, adjectives, and adverbs in general and their functions in particular sentences. b. Form and use regular and irregular plural nouns. c. Use abstract nouns (e.g., *childhood*). d. Form and use regular and irregular verbs. e. Form and use the simple (e.g., *I walked; I walk; I will walk*) verb tenses. f. Ensure subject-verb and pronoun-antecedent agreement.* g. Form and use comparative and superlative adjectives and adverbs, and choose between them depending on what is to be modified. h. Use coordinating and subordinating conjunctions. i. Produce simple, compound, and complex sentences. **j. Write legibly in cursive or joined italics, allowing margins and correct spacing between letters in a word and words in a sentence. CA** **k. Use reciprocal pronouns correctly. CA**	1. Demonstrate command of the conventions of standard English grammar and usage when writing or speaking. a. Use **interrogative,** relative pronouns (*who, whose, whom, which, that*) and relative adverbs (*where, when, why*). **CA** b. Form and use the progressive (e.g., *I was walking; I am walking; I will be walking*) verb tenses. c. Use modal auxiliaries (e.g., *can, may, must*) to convey various conditions. d. Order adjectives within sentences according to conventional patterns (e.g., *a small red bag* rather than *a red small bag*). e. Form and use prepositional phrases. f. Produce complete sentences, recognizing and correcting inappropriate fragments and run-ons.* g. Correctly use frequently confused words (e.g., *to, too, two; there, their*).* **h. Write fluidly and legibly in cursive or joined italics. CA**	1. Demonstrate command of the conventions of standard English grammar and usage when writing or speaking. a. Explain the function of conjunctions, prepositions, and interjections in general and their function in particular sentences. b. Form and use the perfect (e.g., *I had walked; I have walked; I will have walked*) verb tenses. c. Use verb tense to convey various times, sequences, states, and conditions. d. Recognize and correct inappropriate shifts in verb tense.* e. Use correlative conjunctions (e.g., *either/or, neither/nor*).

	Grade 3 Students	Grade 4 Students	Grade 5 Students
Conventions of Standard English (*continued*)	2. Demonstrate command of the conventions of standard English capitalization, punctuation, and spelling when writing. a. Capitalize appropriate words in titles. b. Use commas in addresses. c. Use commas and quotation marks in dialogue. d. Form and use possessives. e. Use conventional spelling for high-frequency and other studied words and for adding suffixes to base words (e.g., *sitting, smiled, cries, happiness*). f. Use spelling patterns and generalizations (e.g., word families, position-based spellings, syllable patterns, ending rules, meaningful word parts) in writing words. g. Consult reference materials, including beginning dictionaries, as needed to check and correct spellings.	2. Demonstrate command of the conventions of standard English capitalization, punctuation, and spelling when writing. a. Use correct capitalization. b. Use commas and quotation marks to mark direct speech and quotations from a text. c. Use a comma before a coordinating conjunction in a compound sentence. d. Spell grade-appropriate words correctly, consulting references as needed.	2. Demonstrate command of the conventions of standard English capitalization, punctuation, and spelling when writing. a. Use punctuation to separate items in a series.* b. Use a comma to separate an introductory element from the rest of the sentence. c. Use a comma to set off the words yes and *no* (e.g., *Yes, thank you*), to set off a tag question from the rest of the sentence (e.g., *It's true, isn't it?*), and to indicate direct address (e.g., *Is that you, Steve?*). d. Use underlining, quotation marks, or italics to indicate titles of works. e. Spell grade-appropriate words correctly, consulting references as needed.
Knowledge of Language	3. Use knowledge of language and its conventions when writing, speaking, reading, or listening. a. Choose words and phrases for effect.* b. Recognize and observe differences between the conventions of spoken and written standard English.	3. Use knowledge of language and its conventions when writing, speaking, reading, or listening. a. Choose words and phrases to convey ideas precisely.* b. Choose punctuation for effect.* c. Differentiate between contexts that call for formal English (e.g., presenting ideas) and situations where informal discourse is appropriate (e.g., small-group discussion).	3. Use knowledge of language and its conventions when writing, speaking, reading, or listening. a. Expand, combine, and reduce sentences for meaning, reader/listener interest, and style. b. Compare and contrast the varieties of English (e.g., dialects, registers) used in stories, dramas, or poems.

	Grade 3 Students	Grade 4 Students	Grade 5 Students
Vocabulary Acquisition and Use	4. Determine or clarify the meaning of unknown and multiple-meaning word and phrases based on *grade 3 reading and content,* choosing flexibly from a range of strategies. a. Use sentence-level context as a clue to the meaning of a word or phrase. b. Determine the meaning of the new word formed when a known affix is added to a known word (e.g., *agreeable/disagreeable, comfortable/ uncomfortable, care/careless, heat/preheat*). c. Use a known root word as a clue to the meaning of an unknown word with the same root (e.g., *company, companion*). d. Use glossaries or beginning dictionaries, both print and digital, to determine or clarify the precise meaning of key words and phrases **in all content areas. CA**	4. Determine or clarify the meaning of unknown and multiple-meaning words and phrases based on *grade 4 reading and content,* choosing flexibly from a range of strategies. a. Use context (e.g., definitions, examples, or restatements in text) as a clue to the meaning of a word or phrase. b. Use common, grade-appropriate Greek and Latin affixes and roots as clues to the meaning of a word (e.g., *telegraph, photograph, autograph*). c. Consult reference materials (e.g., dictionaries, glossaries, thesauruses), both print and digital, to find the pronunciation and determine or clarify the precise meaning of key words and phrases **and to identify alternate word choices in all content areas. CA**	4. Determine or clarify the meaning of unknown and multiple-meaning words and phrases based on *grade 5 reading and content,* choosing flexibly from a range of strategies. a. Use context (e.g., cause/effect relationships and comparisons in text) as a clue to the meaning of a word or phrase. b. Use common, grade-appropriate Greek and Latin affixes and roots as clues to the meaning of a word (e.g., *photograph, photosynthesis*). c. Consult reference materials (e.g., dictionaries, glossaries, thesauruses), both print and digital, to find the pronunciation and determine or clarify the precise meaning of key words and phrases **and to identify alternate word choices in all content areas. CA**
	5. Demonstrate understanding of word relationships and nuances in word meanings. a. Distinguish the literal and non-literal meanings of words and phrases in context (e.g., *take steps*). b. Identify real-life connections between words and their use (e.g., describe people who are *friendly* or *helpful*). c. Distinguish shades of meaning among related words that describe states of mind or degrees of certainty (e.g., *knew, believed, suspected, heard, wondered*).	5. Demonstrate understanding of figurative language, word relationships, and nuances in word meanings. a. Explain the meaning of simple similes and metaphors (e.g., *as pretty as a picture*) in context. b. Recognize and explain the meaning of common idioms, adages, and proverbs. c. Demonstrate understanding of words by relating them to their opposites (antonyms) and to words with similar but not identical meanings (synonyms).	5. Demonstrate understanding of figurative language, word relationships, and nuances in word meanings. a. Interpret figurative language, including similes and metaphors, in context. b. Recognize and explain the meaning of common idioms, adages, and proverbs. c. Use the relationship between particular words (e.g., synonyms, antonyms, homographs) to better understand each of the words.

	Grade 3 Students	Grade 4 Students	Grade 5 Students
Vocabulary Acquisition and Use (continued)	6. Acquire and use accurately grade-appropriate conversational, general academic, and domain-specific words and phrases, including those that signal spatial and temporal relationships (e.g., *After dinner that night we went looking for them*).	6. Acquire and use accurately grade-appropriate general academic and domain-specific words and phrases, including those that signal precise actions, emotions, or states of being (e.g., *quizzed, whined, stammered*) and that are basic to a particular topic (e.g., *wildlife, conservation,* and *endangered* when discussing animal preservation).	6. Acquire and use accurately grade-appropriate general academic and domain-specific words and phrases, including those that signal contrast, addition, and other logical relationships (e.g., *however, although, nevertheless, similarly, moreover, in addition*).

Language Progressive Skills, by Grade

The following skills, marked with an asterisk (*) in Language standards 1–3, are particularly likely to require continued attention in higher grades as they are applied to increasingly sophisticated writing and speaking.

Standard	Grade(s)							
	3	4	5	6	7	8	9–10	11–12
L.3.1f. Ensure subject-verb and pronoun-antecedent agreement.	Yes	Yes	Yes	Yes	Yes	Yes	Yes	Yes
L.3.3a. Choose words and phrases for effect.	Yes	Yes	Yes	Yes	Yes	Yes	Yes	Yes
L.4.1f. Produce complete sentences, recognizing and correcting inappropriate fragments and run-ons.	No	Yes	Yes	Yes	Yes	Yes	Yes	Yes
L.4.1g. Correctly use frequently confused words (e.g., *to/too/two; there/their*).	No	Yes	Yes	Yes	Yes	Yes	Yes	Yes
L.4.3a. Choose words and phrases to convey ideas precisely.*	No	Yes	Yes	Yes	No	No	No	No
L.4.3b. Choose punctuation for effect.	No	Yes	Yes	Yes	Yes	Yes	Yes	Yes
L.5.1d. Recognize and correct inappropriate shifts in verb tense.	No	No	Yes	Yes	Yes	Yes	Yes	Yes
L.5.2a. Use punctuation to separate items in a series.**	No	No	Yes	Yes	Yes	Yes	No	No
L.6.1c. Recognize and correct inappropriate shifts in pronoun number and person.	No	No	No	Yes	Yes	Yes	Yes	Yes
L.6.1d. Recognize and correct vague pronouns (i.e., ones with unclear or ambiguous antecedents).	No	No	No	Yes	Yes	Yes	Yes	Yes
L.6.1e. Recognize variations from standard English in their own and others' writing and speaking, and identify and use strategies to improve expression in conventional language.	No	No	No	Yes	Yes	Yes	Yes	Yes
L.6.2a. Use punctuation (commas, parentheses, dashes) to set off nonrestrictive/parenthetical elements.	No	No	No	Yes	Yes	Yes	Yes	Yes
L.6.3a. Vary sentence patterns for meaning, reader/listener interest, and style.***	No	No	No	Yes	Yes	Yes	Yes	No
L.6.3b. Maintain consistency in style and tone.	No	No	No	Yes	Yes	Yes	Yes	Yes
L.7.1c. Place phrases and clauses within a sentence, recognizing and correcting misplaced and dangling modifiers.	No	No	No	No	Yes	Yes	Yes	Yes
L.7.3a. Choose language that expresses ideas precisely and concisely, recognizing and eliminating wordiness and redundancy.	No	No	No	No	Yes	Yes	Yes	Yes
L.8.1d. Recognize and correct inappropriate shifts in verb voice and mood.	No	No	No	No	No	Yes	Yes	Yes
L.9–10.1a. Use parallel structure.	No	No	No	No	No	No	Yes	Yes

*Subsumed by L.7.3a.
**Subsumed by L.9–10.1a.
***Subsumed by L.11–12.3a.

Standard 10: Range, Quality, and Complexity of Student Reading K–5

Measuring Text Complexity: Three Factors

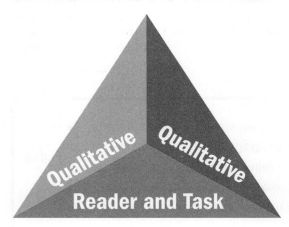

Qualitative evaluation of the text: Levels of meaning, structure, language conventionality and clarity, and knowledge demands

Quantitative evaluation of the text: Readability measures and other scores of text complexity

Matching reader to text and task: Reader variables (such as motivation, knowledge, and experiences) and task variables (such as purpose and the complexity generated by the task assigned and the questions posed)

Note: More detailed information on text complexity and how it is measured is provided in Appendix A.

Range of Text Types for K–5

Students in grades K–5 apply the Reading standards to the following range of text types, with texts selected from a broad range of cultures and periods.

Literature			Informational Text
Stories	**Drama**	**Poetry**	**Literary Nonfiction and Historical, Scientific, and Technical Texts**
Includes children's adventure stories, folktales, legends, fables, fantasy, realistic fiction, and myth.	Includes staged dialogue and brief familiar scenes.	Includes nursery rhymes and the subgenres of the narrative poem, limerick, and free verse poem.	Includes biographies and autobiographies; books about history, social studies, science, and the arts; technical texts, including directions, forms, and information displayed in graphs, charts, or maps; and digital sources on a range of topics.

Texts Illustrating the Complexity, Quality, and Range of Student Reading K–5

	Literature: Stories, Dramas, Poetry	Informational Texts: Literary Nonfiction and Historical, Scientific, and Technical Texts
K†	• *Over in the Meadow* by John Langstaff (traditional) (c1800)* • *A Boy, a Dog, and a Frog* by Mercer Mayer (1967) • *Pancakes for Breakfast* by Tomie DePaola (1978) • *A Story, A Story* by Gail E. Haley (1970)* • *Kitten's First Full Moon* by Kevin Henkes (2004)*	• *My Five Senses* by Aliki (1962)** • *Truck* by Donald Crews (1980) • *I Read Signs* by Tana Hoban (1987) • *What Do You Do With a Tail Like This?* by Steve Jenkins and Robin Page (2003)* • *Amazing Whales!* by Sarah L. Thomson (2005)*
1†	• "Mix a Pancake" by Christina G. Rossetti (1893)** • *Mr. Popper's Penguins* by Richard Atwater (1938)* • *Little Bear* by Else Holmelund Minarik, illustrated by Maurice Sendak (1957)** • *Frog and Toad Together* by Arnold Lobel (1971)** • *Hi! Fly Guy* by Tedd Arnold (2006)	• *A Tree Is a Plant* by Clyde Robert Bulla, illustrated by Stacey Schuett (1960)** • *Starfish* by Edith Thacher Hurd (1962) • *Follow the Water from Brook to Ocean* by Arthur Dorros (1991)** • *From Seed to Pumpkin* by Wendy Pfeffer, illustrated by James Graham Hale (2004)* • *How People Learned to Fly* by Fran Hodgkins and True Kelley (2007)*
2–3	• "Who Has Seen the Wind?" by Christina G. Rossetti (1893) • *Charlotte's Web* by E. B. White (1952)* • *Sarah, Plain and Tall* by Patricia MacLachlan (1985) • *Tops and Bottoms* by Janet Stevens (1995) • *Poppleton in Winter* by Cynthia Rylant, illustrated by Mark Teague (2001)	• *A Medieval Feast* by Aliki (1983) • *From Seed to Plant* by Gail Gibbons (1991) • *The Story of Ruby Bridges* by Robert Coles (1995)* • *A Drop of Water: A Book of Science and Wonder* by Walter Wick (1997) • *Moonshot: The Flight of Apollo 11* by Brian Floca (2009)
4–5	• *Alice's Adventures in Wonderland* by Lewis Carroll (1865) • "Casey at the Bat" by Ernest Lawrence Thayer (1888) • *The Black Stallion* by Walter Farley (1941) • "Zlateh the Goat" by Isaac Bashevis Singer (1984) • *Where the Mountain Meets the Moon* by Grace Lin (2009)	• *Discovering Mars: The Amazing Story of the Red Planet* by Melvin Berger (1992) • *Hurricanes: Earth's Mightiest Storms* by Patricia Lauber (1996) • *A History of US* by Joy Hakim (2005) • *Horses* by Seymour Simon (2006) • *Quest for the Tree Kangaroo: An Expedition to the Cloud Forest of New Guinea* by Sy Montgomery (2006)

*Read-aloud

**Read-along

†Children at the kindergarten and grade 1 levels should be expected to read texts independently that have been specifically written to correlate to their reading level and their word knowledge. Many of the titles listed above are meant to supplement carefully structured independent reading with books to read along with a teacher or that are read aloud to students to build knowledge and cultivate a joy in reading.

Note: Given space limitations, the illustrative texts listed above are meant only to show individual titles that are representative of a wide range of topics and genres. (See Appendix B for excerpts of these and other texts illustrative of K–5 text complexity, quality, and range.) At a curricular or instructional level, within and across grade levels, texts need to be selected around topics or themes that generate knowledge and allow students to study those topics or themes in depth. On the next page is an example of progressions of texts building knowledge across grade levels.

Staying on Topic Within a Grade and Across Grades:
How to Build Knowledge Systematically in English Language Arts K–5

Building knowledge systematically in English language arts is like giving children various pieces of a puzzle in each grade that, over time, will form one big picture. At a curricular or instructional level, texts—within and across grade levels—need to be selected around topics or themes that systematically develop the knowledge base of students. Within a grade level, there should be an adequate number of titles on a single topic that would allow children to study that topic for a sustained period. The knowledge children have learned about particular topics in early grade levels should then be expanded and developed in subsequent grade levels to ensure an increasingly deeper understanding of these topics. Children in the upper elementary grades will generally be expected to read these texts independently and reflect on them in writing. However, children in the early grades (particularly K–2) should participate in rich, structured conversations with an adult in response to the written texts that are read aloud, orally comparing and contrasting as well as analyzing and synthesizing, in the manner called for by the Standards.

Preparation for reading complex informational texts should begin at the very earliest elementary school grades. What follows is one example that uses domain-specific nonfiction titles across grade levels to illustrate how curriculum designers and classroom teachers can infuse the English language arts block with rich, age-appropriate content knowledge and vocabulary in history/social studies, science, and the arts. Having students listen to informational read-alouds in the early grades helps lay the necessary foundation for students' reading and understanding of increasingly complex texts on their own in subsequent grades.

Exemplar Texts on a Topic Across Grades	K	1	2–3	4–5
The Human Body Students can begin learning about the human body starting in kindergarten and then review and extend their learning during each subsequent grade.	**The five senses and associated body parts** • *My Five Senses* by Aliki (1989) • *Hearing* by Maria Rius (1985) • *Sight* by Maria Rius (1985) • *Taste* by Maria Rius (1985) • *Touch* by Maria Rius (1985) **Taking care of your body: Overview (hygiene, diet, exercise, rest)** • *My Amazing Body: A First Look at Health & Fitness* by Pat Thomas (2001) • *Get Up and Go!* By Nancy Carlson (2008) • *Go Wash Up* by Doering Tourville (2008) • *Sleep* by Paul Showers (1997) • *Fuel the Body* by Doering Tourville (2008)	**Introduction to the systems of the human body and associated body parts** • *Under Your Skin: Your Amazing Body* by Mick Manning (2007) • *Me and My Amazing Body* by Joan Sweeney (1999) • *The Human Body* by Gallimard Jeunesse (2007) • *The Busy Body Book* by Lizzy Rockwell (2008) • *First Encyclopedia of the Human Body* by Fiona Chandler (2004) **Taking care of your body: Germs, diseases, and preventing illness** • *Germs Make Me Sick* by Marilyn Berger (1995) • *Tiny Life on Your Body* by Christine Taylor Butler (2005) • *Germ Stories* by Christine Taylor Butler (2005) • *Germ Stories* by Arthur Kornberg (2007) • *All About Scabs* by Genichiro Yagu (1998)	**Digestive and excretory systems** • *What Happens to a Hamburger* by Paul Showers (1985) • *The Digestive System* by Rebecca L. Johnson (2006) • *The Digestive System* by Kristin Petrie (2007) **Taking care of your body: Healthy eating and nutrition** • *Good Enough to Eat* by Lizzy Rockwell (1999) • *Showdown at the Food Pyramid* by Rex Barron (2004) **Muscular, skeletal, and nervous systems** • *The Mighty Muscular and Skeletal Systems* Crabtree Publishing (2009) • *Muscles* by Seymour Simon (1998) • *Bones* by Seymour Simon (1998) • *The Astounding Nervous System* Crabtree Publishing (2009) • *The Nervous System* by Joelle Riley (2004)	**Circulatory system** • *The Heart* by Seymour Simon (2006) • *The Heart and Circulation* by Carol Ballard (2005) • *The Circulatory System* by Kristin Petrie (2007) • *The Amazing Circulatory System* by John Burstein (2009) **Respiratory system** • *The Lungs* by Seymour Simon (2007) • *The Respiratory System* by Susan Glass (2004) • *The Respiratory System* by Kristin Petrie (2007) **Endocrine system** • *The Exciting Endocrine System* by Rebecca Olien (2006) • *The Exciting Endocrine System* by John Burstein (2009)

Standards for

English Language Arts

6–12

College and Career Readiness Anchor Standards for Reading

The grades 6–12 standards on the following pages define what students should understand and be able to do by the end of each grade. They correspond to the College and Career Readiness (CCR) anchor standards below by number. The CCR and grade-specific standards are necessary complements—the former providing broad standards, the latter providing additional specificity—that together define the skills and understandings that all students must demonstrate.

Key Ideas and Details

1. Read closely to determine what the text says explicitly and to make logical inferences from it; cite specific textual evidence when writing or speaking to support conclusions drawn from the text.

2. Determine central ideas or themes of a text and analyze their development; summarize the key supporting details and ideas.

3. Analyze how and why individuals, events, and ideas develop and interact over the course of a text.

Craft and Structure

4. Interpret words and phrases as they are used in a text, including determining technical, connotative, and figurative meanings, and analyze how specific word choices shape meaning or tone.

5. Analyze the structure of texts, including how specific sentences, paragraphs, and larger portions of the text (e.g., a section, chapter, scene, or stanza) relate to each other and the whole.

6. Assess how point of view or purpose shapes the content and style of a text.

---

*Please see "Research to Build and Present Knowledge" in Writing and "Comprehension and Collaboration" in Speaking and Listening for additional standards relevant to gathering, assessing, and applying information from print and digital sources.

Integration of Knowledge and Ideas

7. Integrate and evaluate content presented in diverse media and formats, including visually and quantitatively, as well as in words.*

8. Delineate and evaluate the argument and specific claims in a text, including the validity of the reasoning as well as the relevance and sufficiency of the evidence.

9. Analyze how two or more texts address similar themes or topics in order to build knowledge or to compare the approaches the authors take.

Range of Reading and Level of Text Complexity

10. Read and comprehend complex literary and informational texts independently and proficiently.

Note on range and content of student reading

To become college and career ready, students must grapple with works of exceptional craft and thought whose range extends across genres, cultures, and centuries. Such works offer profound insights into the human condition and serve as models for students' own thinking and writing. Along with high-quality contemporary works, these texts should be chosen from among seminal U.S. documents, the classics of American literature, and the timeless dramas of Shakespeare. Through wide and deep reading of literature and literary nonfiction of steadily increasing sophistication, students gain a reservoir of literary and cultural knowledge, references, and images; the ability to evaluate intricate arguments; and the capacity to surmount the challenges posed by complex texts.

Reading Standards for Literature 6–12

The following standards offer a focus for instruction each year and help ensure that students gain adequate exposure to a range of texts and tasks. Rigor is also infused through the requirement that students read increasingly complex texts through the grades. *Students advancing through the grades are expected to meet each year's grade-specific standards and retain or further develop skills and understandings mastered in preceding grades.*

	Grade 6 Students	Grade 7 Students	Grade 8 Students
Key Ideas and Details	1. Cite textual evidence to support analysis of what the text says explicitly as well as inferences drawn from the text.	1. Cite several pieces of textual evidence to support analysis of what the text says explicitly as well as inferences drawn from the text.	1. Cite the textual evidence that most strongly supports an analysis of what the text says explicitly as well as inferences drawn from the text.
	2. Determine a theme or central idea of a text and how it is conveyed through particular details; provide a summary of the text distinct from personal opinions or judgments.	2. Determine a theme or central idea of a text and analyze its development over the course of the text; provide an objective summary of the text.	2. Determine a theme or central idea of a text and analyze its development over the course of the text, including its relationship to the characters, setting, and plot; provide an objective summary of the text.
	3. Describe how a particular story's or drama's plot unfolds in a series of episodes as well as how the characters respond or change as the plot moves toward a resolution.	3. Analyze how particular elements of a story or drama interact (e.g., how setting shapes the characters or plot).	3. Analyze how particular lines of dialogue or incidents in a story or drama propel the action, reveal aspects of a character, or provoke a decision.
Craft and Structure	4. Determine the meaning of words and phrases as they are used in a text, including figurative and connotative meanings; analyze the impact of a specific word choice on meaning and tone. **(See grade 6 Language standards 4–6 for additional expectations.) CA**	4. Determine the meaning of words and phrases as they are used in a text, including figurative and connotative meanings; analyze the impact of rhymes and other repetitions of sounds (e.g., alliteration) on a specific verse or stanza of a poem or section of a story or drama. **(See grade 7 Language standards 4–6 for additional expectations.) CA**	4. Determine the meaning of words and phrases as they are used in a text, including figurative and connotative meanings; analyze the impact of specific word choices on meaning and tone, including analogies or allusions to other texts. **(See grade 8 Language standards 4–6 for additional expectations.) CA**
	5. Analyze how a particular sentence, chapter, scene, or stanza fits into the overall structure of a text and contributes to the development of the theme, setting, or plot.	5. Analyze how a drama's or poem's form or structure (e.g., soliloquy, sonnet) contributes to its meaning.	5. Compare and contrast the structure of two or more texts and analyze how the differing structure of each text contributes to its meaning and style.
	6. Explain how an author develops the point of view of the narrator or speaker in a text.	6. Analyze how an author develops and contrasts the points of view of different characters or narrators in a text.	6. Analyze how differences in the points of view of the characters and the audience or reader (e.g., created through the use of dramatic irony) create such effects as suspense or humor.

	Grade 6 Students	Grade 7 Students	Grade 8 Students
Integration of Knowledge and Ideas	7. Compare and contrast the experience of reading a story, drama, or poem to listening to or viewing an audio, video, or live version of the text, including contrasting what they "see" and "hear" when reading the text to what they perceive when they listen or watch.	7. Compare and contrast a written story, drama, or poem to its audio, filmed, staged, or multimedia version, analyzing the effects of techniques unique to each medium (e.g., lighting, sound, color, or camera focus and angles in a film).	7. Analyze the extent to which a filmed or live production of a story or drama stays faithful to or departs from the text or script, evaluating the choices made by the director or actors.
	8. (Not applicable to literature)	8. (Not applicable to literature)	8. (Not applicable to literature)
	9. Compare and contrast texts in different forms or genres (e.g., stories and poems; historical novels and fantasy stories) in terms of their approaches to similar themes and topics.	9. Compare and contrast a fictional portrayal of a time, place, or character and a historical account of the same period as a means of understanding how authors of fiction use or alter history.	9. Analyze how a modern work of fiction draws on themes, patterns of events, or character types from myths, traditional stories, or religious works such as the Bible, including describing how the material is rendered new.
Range of Reading and Level of Text Complexity	10. By the end of the year, read and comprehend literature, including stories, dramas, and poems, in the grades 6–8 text complexity band proficiently, with scaffolding as needed at the high end of the range.	10. By the end of the year, read and comprehend literature, including stories, dramas, and poems, in the grades 6–8 text complexity band proficiently, with scaffolding as needed at the high end of the range.	10. By the end of the year, read and comprehend literature, including stories, dramas, and poems, at the high end of grades 6–8 text complexity band independently and proficiently.

Reading Standards for Literature 6–12

The CCR anchor standards and high school grade-specific standards work in tandem to define college and career readiness expectations—the former providing broad standards, the latter providing additional specificity.

	Grades 9–10 Students	Grades 11–12 Students
Key Ideas and Details	1. Cite strong and thorough textual evidence to support analysis of what the text says explicitly as well as inferences drawn from the text.	1. Cite strong and thorough textual evidence to support analysis of what the text says explicitly as well as inferences drawn from the text, including determining where the text leaves matters uncertain.
	2. Determine a theme or central idea of a text and analyze in detail its development over the course of the text, including how it emerges and is shaped and refined by specific details; provide an objective summary of the text.	2. Determine two or more themes or central ideas of a text and analyze their development over the course of the text, including how they interact and build on one another to produce a complex account; provide an objective summary of the text.
	3. Analyze how complex characters (e.g., those with multiple or conflicting motivations) develop over the course of a text, interact with other characters, and advance the plot or develop the theme.	3. Analyze the impact of the author's choices regarding how to develop and relate elements of a story or drama (e.g., where a story is set, how the action is ordered, how the characters/**archetypes** are introduced and developed). **CA**
Craft and Structure	4. Determine the meaning of words and phrases as they are used in the text, including figurative and connotative meanings; analyze the cumulative impact of specific word choices on meaning and tone (e.g., how the language evokes a sense of time and place; how it sets a formal or informal tone). **(See grade 9–10 Language standards 4–6 for additional expectations.) CA**	4. Determine the meaning of words and phrases as they are used in the text, including figurative and connotative meanings; analyze the impact of specific word choices on meaning and tone, including words with multiple meanings or language that is particularly fresh, engaging, or beautiful. (Include Shakespeare as well as other authors.) **(See grade 11–12 Language standards 4–6 for additional expectations.) CA**
	5. Analyze how an author's choices concerning how to structure a text, order events within it (e.g., parallel plots), and manipulate time (e.g., pacing, flashbacks) create such effects as mystery, tension, or surprise.	5. Analyze how an author's choices concerning how to structure specific parts of a text (e.g., the choice of where to begin or end a story, the choice to provide a comedic or tragic resolution) contribute to its overall structure and meaning as well as its aesthetic impact.
	6. Analyze a particular point of view or cultural experience reflected in a work of literature from outside the United States, drawing on a wide reading of world literature.	6. Analyze a case in which grasping point of view requires distinguishing what is directly stated in a text from what is really meant (e.g., satire, sarcasm, irony, or understatement).

	Grades 9–10 Students	Grades 11–12 Students
Integration of Knowledge and Ideas	7. Analyze the representation of a subject or a key scene in two different artistic mediums, including what is emphasized or absent in each treatment (e.g., Auden's "Musée des Beaux Arts" and Breughel's *Landscape with the Fall of Icarus*).	7. Analyze multiple interpretations of a story, drama, or poem (e.g., recorded or live production of a play or recorded novel or poetry), evaluating how each version interprets the source text. (Include at least one play by Shakespeare and one play by an American dramatist.)
	8. (Not applicable to literature)	8. (Not applicable to literature)
	9. Analyze how an author draws on and transforms source material in a specific work (e.g., how Shakespeare treats a theme or topic from Ovid or the Bible or how a later author draws on a play by Shakespeare).	9. Demonstrate knowledge of eighteenth-, nineteenth- and early-twentieth-century foundational works of American literature, including how two or more texts from the same period treat similar themes or topics.
Range of Reading and Level of Text Complexity	10. By the end of grade 9, read and comprehend literature, including stories, dramas, and poems, in the grades 9–10 text complexity band proficiently, with scaffolding as needed at the high end of the range. By the end of grade 10, read and comprehend literature, including stories, dramas, and poems, at the high end of the grades 9–10 text complexity band independently and proficiently.	10. By the end of grade 11, read and comprehend literature, including stories, dramas, and poems, in the grades 11–CCR text complexity band proficiently, with scaffolding as needed at the high end of the range. By the end of grade 12, read and comprehend literature, including stories, dramas, and poems, at the high end of the grades 11–CCR text complexity band independently and proficiently.

Reading Standards for Informational Text 6–12

	Grade 6 Students	Grade 7 Students	Grade 8 Students
Key Ideas and Details	1. Cite textual evidence to support analysis of what the text says explicitly as well as inferences drawn from the text.	1. Cite several pieces of textual evidence to support analysis of what the text says explicitly as well as inferences drawn from the text.	1. Cite the textual evidence that most strongly supports an analysis of what the text says explicitly as well as inferences drawn from the text.
	2. Determine a central idea of a text and how it is conveyed through particular details; provide a summary of the text distinct from personal opinions or judgments.	2. Determine two or more central ideas in a text and analyze their development over the course of the text; provide an objective summary of the text.	2. Determine a central idea of a text and analyze its development over the course of the text, including its relationship to supporting ideas; provide an objective summary of the text.
	3. Analyze in detail how a key individual, event, or idea is introduced, illustrated, and elaborated in a text (e.g., through examples or anecdotes).	3. Analyze the interactions between individuals, events, and ideas in a text (e.g., how ideas influence individuals or events, or how individuals influence ideas or events).	3. Analyze how a text makes connections among and distinctions between individuals, ideas, or events (e.g., through comparisons, analogies, or categories).
Craft and Structure	4. Determine the meaning of words and phrases as they are used in a text, including figurative, connotative, and technical meanings. **(See grade 6 Language standards 4–6 for additional expectations.) CA**	4. Determine the meaning of words and phrases as they are used in a text, including figurative, connotative, and technical meanings; analyze the impact of a specific word choice on meaning and tone. **(See grade 7 Language standards 4–6 for additional expectations.) CA**	4. Determine the meaning of words and phrases as they are used in a text, including figurative, connotative, and technical meanings; analyze the impact of specific word choices on meaning and tone, including analogies or allusions to other texts. **(See grade 8 Language standards 4–6 for additional expectations.) CA**
	5. Analyze how a particular sentence, paragraph, chapter, or section fits into the overall structure of a text and contributes to the development of the ideas. a. **Analyze the use of text features (e.g., graphics, headers, captions) in popular media. CA**	5. Analyze the structure an author uses to organize a text, including how the major sections contribute to the whole and to the development of the ideas. a. **Analyze the use of text features (e.g., graphics, headers, captions) in public documents. CA**	5. Analyze in detail the structure of a specific paragraph in a text, including the role of particular sentences in developing and refining a key concept. a. **Analyze the use of text features (e.g., graphics, headers, captions) in consumer materials. CA**
	6. Determine an author's point of view or purpose in a text and explain how it is conveyed in the text.	6. Determine an author's point of view or purpose in a text and analyze how the author distinguishes his or her position from that of others.	6. Determine an author's point of view or purpose in a text and analyze how the author acknowledges and responds to conflicting evidence or viewpoints.

	Grade 6 Students	Grade 7 Students	Grade 8 Students
Integration of Knowledge and Ideas	7. Integrate information presented in different media or formats (e.g., visually, quantitatively) as well as in words to develop a coherent understanding of a topic or issue.	7. Compare and contrast a text to an audio, video, or multimedia version of the text, analyzing each medium's portrayal of the subject (e.g., how the delivery of a speech affects the impact of the words).	7. Evaluate the advantages and disadvantages of using different mediums (e.g., print or digital text, video, multimedia) to present a particular topic or idea.
	8. Trace and evaluate the argument and specific claims in a text, distinguishing claims that are supported by reasons and evidence from claims that are not.	8. Trace and evaluate the argument and specific claims in a text, assessing whether the reasoning is sound and the evidence is relevant and sufficient to support the claims.	8. Delineate and evaluate the argument and specific claims in a text, assessing whether the reasoning is sound and the evidence is relevant and sufficient; recognize when irrelevant evidence is introduced.
	9. Compare and contrast one author's presentation of events with that of another (e.g., a memoir written by and a biography on the same person).	9. Analyze how two or more authors writing about the same topic shape their presentations of key information by emphasizing different evidence or advancing different interpretations of facts.	9. Analyze a case in which two or more texts provide conflicting information on the same topic and identify where the texts disagree on matters of fact or interpretation.
Range of Reading and Level of Text Complexity	10. By the end of the year, read and comprehend literary nonfiction in the grades 6–8 text complexity band proficiently, with scaffolding as needed at the high end of the range.	10. By the end of the year, read and comprehend literary nonfiction in the grades 6–8 text complexity band proficiently, with scaffolding as needed at the high end of the range.	10. By the end of the year, read and comprehend literary nonfiction at the high end of the grades 6–8 text complexity band independently and proficiently.

Reading Standards for Informational Text 6–12

The CCR anchor standards and high school grade-specific standards work in tandem to define college and career readiness expectations—the former providing broad standards, the latter providing additional specificity.

	Grades 9–10 Students	Grades 11–12 Students
Key Ideas and Details	1. Cite strong and thorough textual evidence to support analysis of what the text says explicitly as well as inferences drawn from the text.	1. Cite strong and thorough textual evidence to support analysis of what the text says explicitly as well as inferences drawn from the text, including determining where the text leaves matters uncertain.
	2. Determine a central idea of a text and analyze its development over the course of the text, including how it emerges and is shaped and refined by specific details; provide an objective summary of the text.	2. Determine two or more central ideas of a text and analyze their development over the course of the text, including how they interact and build on one another to provide a complex analysis; provide an objective summary of the text.
	3. Analyze how the author unfolds an analysis or series of ideas or events, including the order in which the points are made, how they are introduced and developed, and the connections that are drawn between them.	3. Analyze a complex set of ideas or sequence of events and explain how specific individuals, ideas, or events interact and develop over the course of the text.
Craft and Structure	4. Determine the meaning of words and phrases as they are used in a text, including figurative, connotative, and technical meanings; analyze the cumulative impact of specific word choices on meaning and tone (e.g., how the language of a court opinion differs from that of a newspaper). **(See grade 9–10 Language standards 4–6 for additional expectations.) CA**	4. Determine the meaning of words and phrases as they are used in a text, including figurative, connotative, and technical meanings; analyze how an author uses and refines the meaning of a key term or terms over the course of a text (e.g., how Madison defines *faction* in *Federalist* No. 10). **(See grade 11–12 Language standards 4–6 for additional expectations.) CA**
	5. Analyze in detail how an author's ideas or claims are developed and refined by particular sentences, paragraphs, or larger portions of a text (e.g., a section or chapter). a. **Analyze the use of text features (e.g., graphics, headers, captions) in functional workplace documents. CA**	5. Analyze and evaluate the effectiveness of the structure an author uses in his or her exposition or argument, including whether the structure makes points clear, convincing, and engaging. a. **Analyze the use of text features (e.g., graphics, headers, captions) in public documents. CA**
	6. Determine an author's point of view or purpose in a text and analyze how an author uses rhetoric to advance that point of view or purpose.	6. Determine an author's point of view or purpose in a text in which the rhetoric is particularly effective, analyzing how style and content contribute to the power, persuasiveness, or beauty of the text.

	Grades 9–10 Students	Grades 11–12 Students
Integration of Knowledge and Ideas	7. Analyze various accounts of a subject told in different mediums (e.g., a person's life story in both print and multimedia), determining which details are emphasized in each account.	7. Integrate and evaluate multiple sources of information presented in different media or formats (e.g., visually, quantitatively) as well as in words in order to address a question or solve a problem.
	8. Delineate and evaluate the argument and specific claims in a text, assessing whether the reasoning is valid and the evidence is relevant and sufficient; identify false statements and fallacious reasoning.	8. Delineate and evaluate the reasoning in seminal U.S. texts, including the application of constitutional principles and use of legal reasoning (e.g., in U.S. Supreme Court majority opinions and dissents) and the premises, purposes, and arguments in works of public advocacy (e.g., *The Federalist,* presidential addresses).
	9. Analyze seminal U.S. documents of historical and literary significance (e.g., Washington's Farewell Address, the Gettysburg Address, Roosevelt's Four Freedoms speech, King's "Letter from Birmingham Jail"), including how they address related themes and concepts.	9. Analyze seventeenth-, eighteenth-, and nineteenth-century foundational U.S. documents of historical and literary significance (including The Declaration of Independence, the Preamble to the Constitution, the Bill of Rights, and Lincoln's Second Inaugural Address) for their themes, purposes, and rhetorical features.
Range of Reading and Level of Text Complexity	10. By the end of grade 9, read and comprehend literary nonfiction in the grades 9–10 text complexity band proficiently, with scaffolding as needed at the high end of the range. By the end of grade 10, read and comprehend literary nonfiction at the high end of the grades 9–10 text complexity band independently and proficiently.	10. By the end of grade 11, read and comprehend literary nonfiction in the grades 11–CCR text complexity band proficiently, with scaffolding as needed at the high end of the range. By the end of grade 12, read and comprehend literary nonfiction at the high end of the grades 11–CCR text complexity band independently and proficiently.

College and Career Readiness Anchor Standards for Writing

The grades 6–12 standards on the following pages define what students should understand and be able to do by the end of each grade. They correspond to the College and Career Readiness (CCR) anchor standards below by number. The CCR and grade-specific standards are necessary complements—the former providing broad standards, the latter providing additional specificity—that together define the skills and understandings that all students must demonstrate.

Text Types and Purposes*

1. Write arguments to support claims in an analysis of substantive topics or texts, using valid reasoning and relevant and sufficient evidence.

2. Write informative/explanatory texts to examine and convey complex ideas and information clearly and accurately through the effective selection, organization, and analysis of content.

3. Write narratives to develop real or imagined experiences or events using effective technique, well-chosen details, and well-structured event sequences.

Production and Distribution of Writing

4. Produce clear and coherent writing in which the development, organization, and style are appropriate to task, purpose, and audience.

5. Develop and strengthen writing as needed by planning, revising, editing, rewriting, or trying a new approach.

6. Use technology, including the Internet, to produce and publish writing and to interact and collaborate with others.

Research to Build and Present Knowledge

7. Conduct short as well as more sustained research projects based on focused questions, demonstrating understanding of the subject under investigation.

---

*These broad types of writing include many subgenres. See Appendix A for definitions of key writing types.

8. Gather relevant information from multiple print and digital sources, assess the credibility and accuracy of each source, and integrate the information while avoiding plagiarism.

9. Draw evidence from literary and/or informational texts to support analysis, reflection, and research.

Range of Writing

10. Write routinely over extended time frames (time for research, reflection, and revision) and shorter time frames (a single sitting or a day or two) for a range of tasks, purposes, and audiences.

Note on range and content of student writing

For students, writing is a key means of asserting and defending claims, showing what they know about a subject, and conveying what they have experienced, imagined, thought, and felt. To be college- and career-ready writers, students must take task, purpose, and audience into careful consideration, choosing words, information, structures, and formats deliberately. They need to know how to combine elements of different kinds of writing—for example, to use narrative strategies within argument and explanation within narrative—to produce complex and nuanced writing. They need to be able to use technology strategically when creating, refining, and collaborating on writing. They have to become adept at gathering information, evaluating sources, and citing material accurately, reporting findings from their research and analysis of sources in a clear and cogent manner. They must have the flexibility, concentration, and fluency to produce high-quality first-draft text under a tight deadline as well as the capacity to revisit and make improvements to a piece of writing over multiple drafts when circumstances encourage or require it.

Writing Standards 6–12

The following standards for grades 6–12 offer a focus for instruction each year to help ensure that students gain adequate mastery of a range of skills and applications. Each year in their writing, students should demonstrate increasing sophistication in all aspects of language use, from vocabulary and syntax to the development and organization of ideas, and they should address increasingly demanding content and sources. *Students advancing through the grades are expected to meet each year's grade-specific standards and retain or further develop skills and understandings mastered in preceding grades.* The expected growth in student writing ability is reflected both in the standards themselves and in the collection of annotated student writing samples in Appendix C.

	Grade 6 Students	Grade 7 Students	Grade 8 Students
Text Types and Purposes	1. Write arguments to support claims with clear reasons and relevant evidence.	1. Write arguments to support claims with clear reasons and relevant evidence.	1. Write arguments to support claims with clear reasons and relevant evidence.
	a. Introduce claim(s) and organize the reasons and evidence clearly.	a. Introduce claim(s), acknowledge **and address** alternate or opposing claims, and organize the reasons and evidence logically. **CA**	a. Introduce claim(s), acknowledge and distinguish the claim(s) from alternate or opposing claims, and organize the reasons and evidence logically.
	b. Support claim(s) with clear reasons and relevant evidence, using credible sources and demonstrating an understanding of the topic or text.	b. Support claim(s) **or counterarguments** with logical reasoning and relevant evidence, using accurate, credible sources and demonstrating an understanding of the topic or text. **CA**	b. Support claim(s) with logical reasoning and relevant evidence, using accurate, credible sources and demonstrating an understanding of the topic or text.
	c. Use words, phrases, and clauses to clarify the relationships among claim(s) and reasons.	c. Use words, phrases, and clauses to create cohesion and clarify the relationships among claim(s), reasons, and evidence.	c. Use words, phrases, and clauses to create cohesion and clarify the relationships among claim(s), counterclaims, reasons, and evidence.
	d. Establish and maintain a formal style.	d. Establish and maintain a formal style.	d. Establish and maintain a formal style.
	e. Provide a concluding statement or section that follows from the argument presented.	e. Provide a concluding statement or section that follows from and supports the argument presented.	e. Provide a concluding statement or section that follows from and supports the argument presented.

Grade 6 Students	Grade 7 Students	Grade 8 Students

Text Types and Purposes *(continued)*
 	
2. Write informative/explanatory texts to examine a topic and convey ideas, concepts, and information through the selection, organization, and analysis of relevant content.
 	
  a. Introduce a topic **or thesis statement;** organize ideas, concepts, and information, using strategies such as definition, classification, comparison/contrast, and cause/effect; include formatting (e.g., headings), graphics (e.g., charts, tables), and multimedia when useful to aiding comprehension. **CA**
 	
  b. Develop the topic with relevant facts, definitions, concrete details, quotations, or other information and examples.
 	
  c. Use appropriate transitions to clarify the relationships among ideas and concepts.
 	
  d. Use precise language and domain-specific vocabulary to inform about or explain the topic.
 	
  e. Establish and maintain a formal style.
 	
  f. Provide a concluding statement or section that follows from the information or explanation presented.
	2. Write informative/explanatory texts to examine a topic and convey ideas, concepts, and information through the selection, organization, and analysis of relevant content.
	
	  a. Introduce a topic **or thesis statement** clearly, previewing what is to follow; organize ideas, concepts, and information, using strategies such as definition, classification, comparison/contrast, and cause/effect; include formatting (e.g., headings), graphics (e.g., charts, tables), and multimedia when useful to aiding comprehension. **CA**
	
	  b. Develop the topic with relevant facts, definitions, concrete details, quotations, or other information and examples.
	
	  c. Use appropriate transitions to create cohesion and clarify the relationships among ideas and concepts.
	
	  d. Use precise language and domain-specific vocabulary to inform about or explain the topic.
	
	  e. Establish and maintain a formal style.
	
	  f. Provide a concluding statement or section that follows from and supports the information or explanation presented.
		2. Write informative/explanatory texts, **including career development documents (e.g., simple business letters and job applications),** to examine a topic and convey ideas, concepts, and information through the selection, organization, and analysis of relevant content. **CA**
		
		  a. Introduce a topic **or thesis statement** clearly, previewing what is to follow; organize ideas, concepts, and information into broader categories; include formatting (e.g., headings), graphics (e.g., charts, tables), and multimedia when useful to aiding comprehension. **CA**
		
		  b. Develop the topic with relevant, well-chosen facts, definitions, concrete details, quotations, or other information and examples.
		
		  c. Use appropriate and varied transitions to create cohesion and clarify the relationships among ideas and concepts.
		
		  d. Use precise language and domain-specific vocabulary to inform about or explain the topic.
		
		  e. Establish and maintain a formal style.
		
		  f. Provide a concluding statement or section that follows from and supports the information or explanation presented.

Text Types and Purposes (continued)

Grade 6 Students	Grade 7 Students	Grade 8 Students
3. Write narratives to develop real or imagined experiences or events using effective technique, relevant descriptive details, and well-structured event sequences.	3. Write narratives to develop real or imagined experiences or events using effective technique, relevant descriptive details, and well-structured event sequences.	3. Write narratives to develop real or imagined experiences or events using effective technique, relevant descriptive details, and well-structured event sequences.
a. Engage and orient the reader by establishing a context and introducing a narrator and/or characters; organize an event sequence that unfolds naturally and logically.	a. Engage and orient the reader by establishing a context and point of view and introducing a narrator and/or characters; organize an event sequence that unfolds naturally and logically.	a. Engage and orient the reader by establishing a context and point of view and introducing a narrator and/or characters; organize an event sequence that unfolds naturally and logically.
b. Use narrative techniques, such as dialogue, pacing, and description, to develop experiences, events, and/or characters.	b. Use narrative techniques, such as dialogue, pacing, and description, to develop experiences, events, and/or characters.	b. Use narrative techniques, such as dialogue, pacing, description, and reflection, to develop experiences, events, and/or characters.
c. Use a variety of transition words, phrases, and clauses to convey sequence and signal shifts from one time frame or setting to another.	c. Use a variety of transition words, phrases, and clauses to convey sequence and signal shifts from one time frame or setting to another.	c. Use a variety of transition words, phrases, and clauses to convey sequence, signal shifts from one time frame or setting to another, and show the relationships among experiences and events.
d. Use precise words and phrases, relevant descriptive details, and sensory language to convey experiences and events.	d. Use precise words and phrases, relevant descriptive details, and sensory language to capture the action and convey experiences and events.	d. Use precise words and phrases, relevant descriptive details, and sensory language to capture the action and convey experiences and events.
e. Provide a conclusion that follows from the narrated experiences or events.	e. Provide a conclusion that follows from and reflects on the narrated experiences or events.	e. Provide a conclusion that follows from and reflects on the narrated experiences or events.

	Grade 6 Students	Grade 7 Students	Grade 8 Students
Production and Distribution of Writing	4. Produce clear and coherent writing in which the development, organization, and style are appropriate to task, purpose, and audience. (Grade-specific expectations for writing types are defined in standards 1–3 above.)	4. Produce clear and coherent writing in which the development, organization, and style are appropriate to task, purpose, and audience. (Grade-specific expectations for writing types are defined in standards 1–3 above.)	4. Produce clear and coherent writing in which the development, organization, and style are appropriate to task, purpose, and audience. (Grade-specific expectations for writing types are defined in standards 1–3 above.)
	5. With some guidance and support from peers and adults, develop and strengthen writing as needed by planning, revising, editing, rewriting, or trying a new approach. (Editing for conventions should demonstrate command of Language standards 1–3 up to and including grade 6.)	5. With some guidance and support from peers and adults, develop and strengthen writing as needed by planning, revising, editing, rewriting, or trying a new approach, focusing on how well purpose and audience have been addressed. (Editing for conventions should demonstrate command of Language standards 1–3 up to and including grade 7.)	5. With some guidance and support from peers and adults, develop and strengthen writing as needed by planning, revising, editing, rewriting, or trying a new approach, focusing on how well purpose and audience have been addressed. (Editing for conventions should demonstrate command of Language standards 1–3 up to and including grade 8.)
	6. Use technology, including the Internet, to produce and publish writing as well as to interact and collaborate with others; demonstrate sufficient command of keyboarding skills to type a minimum of three pages in a single sitting.	6. Use technology, including the Internet, to produce and publish writing and link to and cite sources as well as to interact and collaborate with others, including linking to and citing sources.	6. Use technology, including the Internet, to produce and publish writing and present the relationships between information and ideas efficiently as well as to interact and collaborate with others.
Research to Build and Present Knowledge	7. Conduct short research projects to answer a question, drawing on several sources and refocusing the inquiry when appropriate.	7. Conduct short research projects to answer a question, drawing on several sources and generating additional related, focused questions for further research and investigation.	7. Conduct short research projects to answer a question (including a self-generated question), drawing on several sources and generating additional related, focused questions that allow for multiple avenues of exploration.
	8. Gather relevant information from multiple print and digital sources; assess the credibility of each source; and quote or paraphrase the data and conclusions of others while avoiding plagiarism and providing basic bibliographic information for sources.	8. Gather relevant information from multiple print and digital sources, using search terms effectively; assess the credibility and accuracy of each source; and quote or paraphrase the data and conclusions of others while avoiding plagiarism and following a standard format for citation.	8. Gather relevant information from multiple print and digital sources, using search terms effectively; assess the credibility and accuracy of each source; and quote or paraphrase the data and conclusions of others while avoiding plagiarism and following a standard format for citation.

Grade 6 Students	Grade 7 Students	Grade 8 Students
Research to Build and Present Knowledge (continued) 9. Draw evidence from literary or informational texts to support analysis, reflection, and research. a. Apply *grade 6 Reading standards* to literature (e.g., "Compare and contrast texts in different forms or genres [e.g., stories and poems; historical novels and fantasy stories] in terms of their approaches to similar themes and topics"). b. Apply *grade 6 Reading standards* to literary nonfiction (e.g., "Trace and evaluate the argument and specific claims in a text, distinguishing claims that are supported by reasons and evidence from claims that are not").	9. Draw evidence from literary or informational texts to support analysis, reflection, and research. a. Apply *grade 7 Reading standards* to literature (e.g., "Compare and contrast a fictional portrayal of a time, place, or character and a historical account of the same period as a means of understanding how authors of fiction use or alter history"). b. Apply *grade 7 Reading standards* to literary nonfiction (e.g. "Trace and evaluate the argument and specific claims in a text, assessing whether the reasoning is sound and the evidence is relevant and sufficient to support the claims").	9. Draw evidence from literary or informational texts to support analysis, reflection, and research. a. Apply *grade 8 Reading standards* to literature (e.g., "Analyze how a modern work of fiction draws on themes, patterns of events, or character types from myths, traditional stories, or religious works such as the Bible, including describing how the material is rendered new"). b. Apply *grade 8 Reading standards* to literary nonfiction (e.g., "Delineate and evaluate the argument and specific claims in a text, assessing whether the reasoning is sound and the evidence is relevant and sufficient; recognize when irrelevant evidence is introduced").
Range of Writing 10. Write routinely over extended time frames (time for research, reflection, and revision) and shorter time frames (a single sitting or a day or two) for a range of discipline-specific tasks, purposes, and audiences.	10. Write routinely over extended time frames (time for research, reflection, and revision) and shorter time frames (a single sitting or a day or two) for a range of discipline-specific tasks, purposes, and audiences.	10. Write routinely over extended time frames (time for research, reflection, and revision) and shorter time frames (a single sitting or a day or two) for a range of discipline-specific tasks, purposes, and audiences.

Writing Standards 6–12

The CCR anchor standards and high school grade-specific standards work in tandem to define college and career readiness expectations—the former providing broad standards, the latter providing additional specificity.

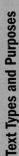

Grades 9–10 Students	Grades 11–12 Students
Text Types and Purposes	
1. Write arguments to support claims in an analysis of substantive topics or texts, using valid reasoning and relevant and sufficient evidence.	1. Write arguments to support claims in an analysis of substantive topics or texts, using valid reasoning and relevant and sufficient evidence.
a. Introduce precise claim(s), distinguish the claim(s) from alternate or opposing claims, and create an organization that establishes clear relationships among claim(s), counterclaims, reasons, and evidence.	a. Introduce precise, knowledgeable claim(s), establish the significance of the claim(s), distinguish the claim(s) from alternate or opposing claims, and create an organization that logically sequences claim(s), counterclaims, reasons, and evidence.
b. Develop claim(s) and counterclaims fairly, supplying evidence for each while pointing out the strengths and limitations of both in a manner that anticipates the audience's knowledge level and concerns.	b. Develop claim(s) and counterclaims fairly and thoroughly, supplying the most relevant evidence for each while pointing out the strengths and limitations of both in a manner that anticipates the audience's knowledge level, concerns, values, and possible biases.
c. Use words, phrases, and clauses to link the major sections of the text, create cohesion, and clarify the relationships between claim(s) and reasons, between reasons and evidence, and between claim(s) and counterclaims.	c. Use words, phrases, and clauses as well as varied syntax to link the major sections of the text, create cohesion, and clarify the relationships between claim(s) and reasons, between reasons and evidence, and between claim(s) and counterclaims.
d. Establish and maintain a formal style and objective tone while attending to the norms and conventions of the discipline in which they are writing.	d. Establish and maintain a formal style and objective tone while attending to the norms and conventions of the discipline in which they are writing.
e. Provide a concluding statement or section that follows from and supports the argument presented.	e. Provide a concluding statement or section that follows from and supports the argument presented.
	f. Use specific rhetorical devices to support assertions (e.g., appeal to logic through reasoning; appeal to emotion or ethical belief; relate a personal anecdote, case study, or analogy). CA

Grades 9–10 Students	Grades 11–12 Students
2. Write informative/explanatory texts to examine and convey complex ideas, concepts, and information clearly and accurately through the effective selection, organization, and analysis of content.	2. Write informative/explanatory texts to examine and convey complex ideas, concepts, and information clearly and accurately through the effective selection, organization, and analysis of content.
a. Introduce a topic **or thesis statement**; organize complex ideas, concepts, and information to make important connections and distinctions; include formatting (e.g., headings), graphics (e.g., figures, tables), and multimedia when useful to aiding comprehension. **CA**	a. Introduce a topic **or thesis statement**; organize complex ideas, concepts, and information so that each new element builds on that which precedes it to create a unified whole; include formatting (e.g., headings), graphics (e.g., figures, tables), and multimedia when useful to aiding comprehension. **CA**
b. Develop the topic with well-chosen, relevant, and sufficient facts, extended definitions, concrete details, quotations, or other information and examples appropriate to the audience's knowledge of the topic.	b. Develop the topic thoroughly by selecting the most significant and relevant facts, extended definitions, concrete details, quotations, or other information and examples appropriate to the audience's knowledge of the topic.
c. Use appropriate and varied transitions to link the major sections of the text, create cohesion, and clarify the relationships among complex ideas and concepts.	c. Use appropriate and varied transitions and syntax to link the major sections of the text, create cohesion, and clarify the relationships among complex ideas and concepts.
d. Use precise language and domain-specific vocabulary to manage the complexity of the topic.	d. Use precise language, domain-specific vocabulary, and techniques such as metaphor, simile, and analogy to manage the complexity of the topic.
e. Establish and maintain a formal style and objective tone while attending to the norms and conventions of the discipline in which they are writing.	e. Establish and maintain a formal style and objective tone while attending to the norms and conventions of the discipline in which they are writing.
f. Provide a concluding statement or section that follows from and supports the information or explanation presented (e.g., articulating implications or the significance of the topic).	f. Provide a concluding statement or section that follows from and supports the information or explanation presented (e.g., articulating implications or the significance of the topic).

Text Types and Purposes (continued)

	Grades 9–10 Students	Grades 11–12 Students
Text Types and Purposes *(continued)*	3. Write narratives to develop real or imagined experiences or events using effective technique, well-chosen details, and well-structured event sequences. a. Engage and orient the reader by setting out a problem, situation, or observation, establishing one or multiple point(s) of view, and introducing a narrator and/or characters; create a smooth progression of experiences or events. b. Use narrative techniques, such as dialogue, pacing, description, reflection, and multiple plot lines, to develop experiences, events, and/or characters. c. Use a variety of techniques to sequence events so that they build on one another to create a coherent whole. d. Use precise words and phrases, telling details, and sensory language to convey a vivid picture of the experiences, events, setting, and/or characters. e. Provide a conclusion that follows from and reflects on what is experienced, observed, or resolved over the course of the narrative.	3. Write narratives to develop real or imagined experiences or events using effective technique, well-chosen details, and well-structured event sequences. a. Engage and orient the reader by setting out a problem, situation, or observation and its significance, establishing one or multiple point(s) of view, and introducing a narrator and/or characters; create a smooth progression of experiences or events. b. Use narrative techniques, such as dialogue, pacing, description, reflection, and multiple plot lines, to develop experiences, events, and/or characters. c. Use a variety of techniques to sequence events so that they build on one another to create a coherent whole and build toward a particular tone and outcome (e.g., a sense of mystery, suspense, growth, or resolution). d. Use precise words and phrases, telling details, and sensory language to convey a vivid picture of the experiences, events, setting, and/or characters. e. Provide a conclusion that follows from and reflects on what is experienced, observed, or resolved over the course of the narrative.
Production and Distribution of Writing	4. Produce clear and coherent writing in which the development, organization, and style are appropriate to task, purpose, and audience. (Grade-specific expectations for writing types are defined in standards 1–3 above.)	4. Produce clear and coherent writing in which the development, organization, and style are appropriate to task, purpose, and audience. (Grade-specific expectations for writing types are defined in standards 1–3 above.)
	5. Develop and strengthen writing as needed by planning, revising, editing, rewriting, or trying a new approach, focusing on addressing what is most significant for a specific purpose and audience. (Editing for conventions should demonstrate command of Language standards 1–3 up to and including grades 9–10.)	5. Develop and strengthen writing as needed by planning, revising, editing, rewriting, or trying a new approach, focusing on addressing what is most significant for a specific purpose and audience. (Editing for conventions should demonstrate command of Language standards 1–3 up to and including grades 11–12.)
	6. Use technology, including the Internet, to produce, publish, and update individual or shared writing products, taking advantage of technology's capacity to link to other information and to display information flexibly and dynamically.	6. Use technology, including the Internet, to produce, publish, and update individual or shared writing products in response to ongoing feedback, including new arguments or information.

	Grades 9–10 Students	Grades 11–12 Students
Research to Build and Present Knowledge	7. Conduct short as well as more sustained research projects to answer a question (including a self-generated question) or solve a problem; narrow or broaden the inquiry when appropriate; synthesize multiple sources on the subject, demonstrating understanding of the subject under investigation.	7. Conduct short as well as more sustained research projects to answer a question (including a self-generated question) or solve a problem; narrow or broaden the inquiry when appropriate; synthesize multiple sources on the subject, demonstrating understanding of the subject under investigation.
	8. Gather relevant information from multiple authoritative print and digital sources, using advanced searches effectively; assess the usefulness of each source in answering the research question; integrate information into the text selectively to maintain the flow of ideas, avoiding plagiarism and following a standard format for citation **including footnotes and endnotes. CA**	8. Gather relevant information from multiple authoritative print and digital sources, using advanced searches effectively; assess the strengths and limitations of each source in terms of the task, purpose, and audience; integrate information into the text selectively to maintain the flow of ideas, avoiding plagiarism and overreliance on any one source and following a standard format for citation **including footnotes and endnotes. CA**
	9. Draw evidence from literary or informational texts to support analysis, reflection, and research. a. Apply *grades 9–10 Reading standards* to literature (e.g., "Analyze how an author draws on and transforms source material in a specific work [e.g., how Shakespeare treats a theme or topic from Ovid or the Bible or how a later author draws on a play by Shakespeare]"). b. Apply *grades 9–10 Reading standards* to literary nonfiction (e.g., "Delineate and evaluate the argument and specific claims in a text, assessing whether the reasoning is valid and the evidence is relevant and sufficient; identify false statements and fallacious reasoning").	9. Draw evidence from literary or informational texts to support analysis, reflection, and research. a. Apply *grades 11–12 Reading standards* to literature (e.g., "Demonstrate knowledge of eighteenth-, nineteenth- and early-twentieth-century foundational works of American literature, including how two or more texts from the same period treat similar themes or topics"). b. Apply *grades 11–12 Reading standards* to literary nonfiction (e.g., "Delineate and evaluate the reasoning in seminal U.S. texts, including the application of constitutional principles and use of legal reasoning [e.g., in U.S. Supreme Court Case majority opinions and dissents] and the premises, purposes, and arguments in works of public advocacy [e.g., *The Federalist*, presidential addresses]").
Range of Writing	10. Write routinely over extended time frames (time for research, reflection, and revision) and shorter time frames (a single sitting or a day or two) for a range of tasks, purposes, and audiences.	10. Write routinely over extended time frames (time for research, reflection, and revision) and shorter time frames (a single sitting or a day or two) for a range of tasks, purposes, and audiences.

College and Career Readiness Anchor Standards for Speaking and Listening

The grades 6–12 standards on the following pages define what students should understand and be able to do by the end of each grade. They correspond to the College and Career Readiness (CCR) anchor standards below by number. The CCR and grade-specific standards are necessary complements—the former providing broad standards, the latter providing additional specificity—that together define the skills and understandings that all students must demonstrate.

Comprehension and Collaboration

1. Prepare for and participate effectively in a range of conversations and collaborations with diverse partners, building on others' ideas and expressing their own clearly and persuasively.

2. Integrate and evaluate information presented in diverse media and formats, including visually, quantitatively, and orally.

3. Evaluate a speaker's point of view, reasoning, and use of evidence and rhetoric.

Presentation of Knowledge and Ideas

4. Present information, findings, and supporting evidence such that listeners can follow the line of reasoning and the organization, development, and style are appropriate to task, purpose, and audience.

5. Make strategic use of digital media and visual displays of data to express information and enhance understanding of presentations.

6. Adapt speech to a variety of contexts and communicative tasks, demonstrating command of formal English when indicated or appropriate.

Note on range and content of student speaking and listening

To be college and career ready, students must have ample opportunities to take part in a variety of rich, structured conversations—as part of a whole class, in small groups, and with a partner—built around important content in various domains. They must be able to contribute appropriately to these conversations, make comparisons and contrasts, and analyze and synthesize a multitude of ideas according to the standards of evidence appropriate to a particular discipline. Whatever their intended major or profession, high school graduates will depend heavily on their ability to listen attentively to others so that they are able to build on others' meritorious ideas while expressing their own clearly and persuasively.

New technologies have broadened and expanded the role that speaking and listening play in acquiring and sharing knowledge and have tightened the link to other forms of communication. The Internet has accelerated the speed at which connections between speaking, listening, reading, and writing can be made, requiring that students be ready to use these modalities nearly simultaneously. Technology itself is changing quickly, creating a new urgency for students to be adaptable in response to change.

Speaking and Listening Standards 6–12

SL

The following standards for grades 6–12 offer a focus for instruction in each year to help ensure that students gain adequate mastery of a range of skills and applications. *Students advancing through the grades are expected to meet each year's grade-specific standards and retain or further develop skills and understandings mastered in preceding grades.*

	Grade 6 Students	Grade 7 Students	Grade 8 Students
Comprehension and Collaboration	1. Engage effectively in a range of collaborative discussions (one-on-one, in groups, and teacher-led) with diverse partners on *grade 6 topics, texts, and issues,* building on others' ideas and expressing their own clearly. a. Come to discussions prepared, having read or studied required material; explicitly draw on that preparation by referring to evidence on the topic, text, or issue to probe and reflect on ideas under discussion. b. Follow rules for collegial discussions, set specific goals and deadlines, and define individual roles as needed. c. Pose and respond to specific questions with elaboration and detail by making comments that contribute to the topic, text, or issue under discussion. d. Review the key ideas expressed and demonstrate understanding of multiple perspectives through reflection and paraphrasing.	1. Engage effectively in a range of collaborative discussions (one-on-one, in groups, and teacher-led) with diverse partners on *grade 7 topics, texts, and issues,* building on others' ideas and expressing their own clearly. a. Come to discussions prepared, having read or researched material under study; explicitly draw on that preparation by referring to evidence on the topic, text, or issue to probe and reflect on ideas under discussion. b. Follow rules for collegial discussions, track progress toward specific goals and deadlines, and define individual roles as needed. c. Pose questions that elicit elaboration and respond to others' questions and comments with relevant observations and ideas that bring the discussion back on topic as needed. d. Acknowledge new information expressed by others and, when warranted, modify their own views.	1. Engage effectively in a range of collaborative discussions (one-on-one, in groups, and teacher-led) with diverse partners on *grade 8 topics, texts, and issues,* building on others' ideas and expressing their own clearly. a. Come to discussions prepared, having read or researched material under study; explicitly draw on that preparation by referring to evidence on the topic, text, or issue to probe and reflect on ideas under discussion. b. Follow rules for collegial discussions and decision-making, track progress toward specific goals and deadlines, and define individual roles as needed. c. Pose questions that connect the ideas of several speakers and respond to others' questions and comments with relevant evidence, observations, and ideas. d. Acknowledge new information expressed by others, and, when warranted, qualify or justify their own views in light of the evidence presented.
	2. Interpret information presented in diverse media and formats (e.g., visually, quantitatively, orally) and explain how it contributes to a topic, text, or issue under study.	2. Analyze the main ideas and supporting details presented in diverse media and formats (e.g., visually, quantitatively, orally) and explain how the ideas clarify a topic, text, or issue under study.	2. Analyze the purpose of information presented in diverse media and formats (e.g., visually, quantitatively, orally) and evaluate the motives (e.g., social, commercial, political) behind its presentation.
	3. Delineate a speaker's argument and specific claims, distinguishing claims that are supported by reasons and evidence from claims that are not.	3. Delineate a speaker's argument and specific claims, **and attitude toward the subject,** evaluating the soundness of the reasoning and the relevance and sufficiency of the evidence. **CA**	3. Delineate a speaker's argument and specific claims, evaluating the soundness of the reasoning and relevance and sufficiency of the evidence and identifying when irrelevant evidence is introduced.

	Grade 6 Students	Grade 7 Students	Grade 8 Students

Presentation of Knowledge and Ideas	4. Present claims and findings (**e.g., argument, narrative, informative, response to literature presentations**), sequencing ideas logically and using pertinent descriptions, facts, and details **and nonverbal elements** to accentuate main ideas or themes; use appropriate eye contact, adequate volume, and clear pronunciation. **CA**
	
	  a. **Plan and deliver an informative/explanatory presentation that: develops a topic with relevant facts, definitions, and concrete details; uses appropriate transitions to clarify relationships; uses precise language and domain specific vocabulary; and provides a strong conclusion. CA**
		4. Present claims and findings (**e.g., argument, narrative, summary presentations**), emphasizing salient points in a focused, coherent manner with pertinent descriptions, facts, details, and examples; use appropriate eye contact, adequate volume, and clear pronunciation. **CA**
		
		  a. **Plan and present an argument that: supports a claim, acknowledges counterarguments, organizes evidence logically, uses words and phrases to create cohesion, and provides a concluding statement that supports the argument presented. CA**
			4. Present claims and findings (**e.g., argument, narrative, response to literature presentations**), emphasizing salient points in a focused, coherent manner with relevant evidence, sound valid reasoning, and well-chosen details; use appropriate eye contact, adequate volume, and clear pronunciation. **CA**
			
			  a. **Plan and present a narrative that: establishes a context and point of view, presents a logical sequence, uses narrative techniques (e.g., dialogue, pacing, description, sensory language), uses a variety of transitions, and provides a conclusion that reflects the experience. CA**

	5. Include multimedia components (e.g., graphics, images, music, sound) and visual displays in presentations to clarify information.	5. Include multimedia components and visual displays in presentations to clarify claims and findings and emphasize salient points.	5. Integrate multimedia and visual displays into presentations to clarify information, strengthen claims and evidence, and add interest.
	6. Adapt speech to a variety of contexts and tasks, demonstrating command of formal English when indicated or appropriate. (See grade 6 Language standards 1 and 3 for specific expectations.)	6. Adapt speech to a variety of contexts and tasks, demonstrating command of formal English when indicated or appropriate. (See grade 7 Language standards 1 and 3 for specific expectations.)	6. Adapt speech to a variety of contexts and tasks, demonstrating command of formal English when indicated or appropriate. (See grade 8 Language standards 1 and 3 for specific expectations.)

SL

Speaking and Listening Standards 6–12

The CCR anchor standards and high school grade-specific standards work in tandem to define college and career readiness expectations—the former providing broad standards, the latter providing additional specificity.

Grades 9–10 Students	Grades 11–12 Students
Comprehension and Collaboration	
1. Initiate and participate effectively in a range of collaborative discussions (one-on-one, in groups, and teacher-led) with diverse partners on *grades 9–10 topics, texts, and issues,* building on others' ideas and expressing their own clearly and persuasively.	1. Initiate and participate effectively in a range of collaborative discussions (one-on- one, in groups, and teacher-led) with diverse partners on *grades 11–12 topics, texts, and issues,* building on others' ideas and expressing their own clearly and persuasively.
a. Come to discussions prepared, having read and researched material under study; explicitly draw on that preparation by referring to evidence from texts and other research on the topic or issue to stimulate a thoughtful, well-reasoned exchange of ideas.	a. Come to discussions prepared, having read and researched material under study; explicitly draw on that preparation by referring to evidence from texts and other research on the topic or issue to stimulate a thoughtful, well-reasoned exchange of ideas.
b. Work with peers to set rules for collegial discussions and decision-making (e.g., informal consensus, taking votes on key issues, presentation of alternate views), clear goals and deadlines, and individual roles as needed.	b. Work with peers to promote civil, democratic discussions and decision-making, set clear goals and deadlines, and establish individual roles as needed.
c. Propel conversations by posing and responding to questions that relate the current discussion to broader themes or larger ideas; actively incorporate others into the discussion; and clarify, verify, or challenge ideas and conclusions.	c. Propel conversations by posing and responding to questions that probe reasoning and evidence; ensure a hearing for a full range of positions on a topic or issue; clarify, verify, or challenge ideas and conclusions; and promote divergent and creative perspectives.
d. Respond thoughtfully to diverse perspectives, summarize points of agreement and disagreement, and, when warranted, qualify or justify their own views and understanding and make new connections in light of the evidence and reasoning presented.	d. Respond thoughtfully to diverse perspectives; synthesize comments, claims, and evidence made on all sides of an issue; resolve contradictions when possible; and determine what additional information or research is required to deepen the investigation or complete the task.
2. Integrate multiple sources of information presented in diverse media or formats (e.g., visually, quantitatively, orally) evaluating the credibility and accuracy of each source.	2. Integrate multiple sources of information presented in diverse formats and media (e.g., visually, quantitatively, orally) in order to make informed decisions and solve problems, evaluating the credibility and accuracy of each source and noting any discrepancies among the data.
3. Evaluate a speaker's point of view, reasoning, and use of evidence and rhetoric, identifying any fallacious reasoning or exaggerated or distorted evidence.	3. Evaluate a speaker's point of view, reasoning, and use of evidence and rhetoric, assessing the stance, premises, links among ideas, word choice, points of emphasis, and tone used.

Grades 9–10 Students	Grades 11–12 Students
4. Present information, findings, and supporting evidence clearly, concisely, and logically **(using appropriate eye contact, adequate volume, and clear pronunciation)** such that listeners can follow the line of reasoning and the organization, development, substance, and style are appropriate to purpose (e.g., **argument, narrative, informative, response to literature presentations**), audience, and task. **CA** a. Plan and deliver an informative/explanatory presentation that: presents evidence in support of a thesis, conveys information from primary and secondary sources coherently, uses domain specific vocabulary, and provides a conclusion that summarizes the main points. (9th or 10th grade) **CA** b. Plan, memorize, and present a recitation (e.g., poem, selection from a speech or dramatic soliloquy) that: conveys the meaning of the selection and includes appropriate performance techniques (e.g., tone, rate, voice modulation) to achieve the desired aesthetic effect. (9th or 10th grade) **CA**	**4.** Present information, findings, and supporting evidence (e.g., **reflective, historical investigation, response to literature presentations**), conveying a clear and distinct perspective **and a logical argument,** such that listeners can follow the line of reasoning, alternative or opposing perspectives are addressed, and the organization, development, substance, and style are appropriate to purpose, audience, and a range of formal and informal tasks. **Use appropriate eye contact, adequate volume, and clear pronunciation. CA** a. Plan and deliver a reflective narrative that: explores the significance of a personal experience, event, or concern; uses sensory language to convey a vivid picture; includes appropriate narrative techniques (e.g., dialogue, pacing, description); and draws comparisons between the specific incident and broader themes. (11th or 12th grade) **CA** b. Plan and present an argument that: supports a precise claim; provides a logical sequence for claims, counterclaims, and evidence; uses rhetorical devices to support assertions (e.g., analogy, appeal to logic through reasoning, appeal to emotion or ethical belief); uses varied syntax to link major sections of the presentation to create cohesion and clarity; and provides a concluding statement that supports the argument presented. (11th or 12th grade) **CA**
5. Make strategic use of digital media (e.g., textual, graphical, audio, visual, and interactive elements) in presentations to enhance understanding of findings, reasoning, and evidence and to add interest.	**5.** Make strategic use of digital media (e.g., textual, graphical, audio, visual, and interactive elements) in presentations to enhance understanding of findings, reasoning, and evidence and to add interest.
6. Adapt speech to a variety of contexts and tasks, demonstrating command of formal English when indicated or appropriate. (See grades 9–10 Language standards 1 and 3 for specific expectations.)	**6.** Adapt speech to a variety of contexts and tasks, demonstrating a command of formal English when indicated or appropriate. (See grades 11–12 Language standards 1 and 3 for specific expectations.)

Presentation of Knowledge and Ideas

College and Career Readiness Anchor Standards for Language

The grades 6–12 standards on the following pages define what students should understand and be able to do by the end of each grade. They correspond to the College and Career Readiness (CCR) anchor standards below by number. The CCR and grade-specific standards are necessary complements—the former providing broad standards, the latter providing additional specificity—that together define the skills and understandings that all students must demonstrate.

Conventions of Standard English

1. Demonstrate command of the conventions of standard English grammar and usage when writing or speaking.

2. Demonstrate command of the conventions of standard English capitalization, punctuation, and spelling when writing.

Knowledge of Language

3. Apply knowledge of language to understand how language functions in different contexts, to make effective choices for meaning or style, and to comprehend more fully when reading or listening.

Vocabulary Acquisition and Use

4. Determine or clarify the meaning of unknown and multiple-meaning words and phrases by using context clues, analyzing meaningful word parts, and consulting general and specialized reference materials, as appropriate.

5. Demonstrate understanding of figurative language, word relationships, and nuances in word meanings.

6. Acquire and use accurately a range of general academic and domain-specific words and phrases sufficient for reading, writing, speaking, and listening at the college- and career-readiness level; demonstrate independence in gathering vocabulary knowledge when encountering an unknown term important to comprehension or expression.

Note on range and content of student language use

To be college and career ready in language, students must have firm control over the conventions of standard English. At the same time, they must come to appreciate that language is as at least as much a matter of craft as of rules and be able to choose words, syntax, and punctuation to express themselves and achieve particular functions and rhetorical effects. They must also have extensive vocabularies, built through reading and study, enabling them to comprehend complex texts and engage in purposeful writing about and conversations around content. They need to become skilled in determining or clarifying the meaning of words and phrases they encounter, choosing flexibly from an array of strategies to aid them. They must learn to see an individual word as part of a network of other words— words, for example, that have similar denotations but different connotations. The inclusion of Language standards in its own strand should not be taken as an indication that skills related to conventions, effective language use, and vocabulary are unimportant to reading, writing, speaking, and listening; indeed, they are inseparable from such contexts.

Language Standards 6–12

The following standards for grades 6–12 offer a focus for instruction each year to help ensure that students gain adequate mastery of a range of skills and applications. *Students advancing through the grades are expected to meet each year's grade-specific standards and retain or further develop skills and understandings mastered in preceding grades.* Beginning in grade 3, skills and understandings that are particularly likely to require continued attention in higher grades as they are applied to increasingly sophisticated writing and speaking are marked with an asterisk (*). See the "Language Progressive Skills, by Grade" table on page 76 for a complete listing and Appendix A for an example of how these skills develop in sophistication.

	Grade 6 Students	Grade 7 Students	Grade 8 Students
Conventions of Standards English	1. Demonstrate command of the conventions of standard English grammar and usage when writing or speaking. a. Ensure that pronouns are in the proper case (subjective, objective, possessive). b. Use **all pronouns, including** intensive pronouns (e.g., *myself, ourselves*) **correctly. CA** c. Recognize and correct inappropriate shifts in pronoun number and person.* d. Recognize and correct vague pronouns (i.e., ones with unclear or ambiguous antecedents).* e. Recognize variations from standard English in their own and others' writing and speaking, and identify and use strategies to improve expression in conventional language.*	1. Demonstrate command of the conventions of standard English grammar and usage when writing or speaking. a. Explain the function of phrases and clauses in general and their function in specific sentences. b. Choose among simple, compound, complex, and compound-complex sentences to signal differing relationships among ideas. c. Place phrases and clauses within a sentence, recognizing and correcting misplaced and dangling modifiers.*	1. Demonstrate command of the conventions of standard English grammar and usage when writing or speaking. a. Explain the function of verbals (gerunds, participles, infinitives) in general and their function in particular sentences. b. Form and use verbs in the active and passive voice. c. Form and use verbs in the indicative, imperative, interrogative, conditional, and subjunctive mood. d. Recognize and correct inappropriate shifts in verb voice and mood.*
	2. Demonstrate command of the conventions of standard English capitalization, punctuation, and spelling when writing. a. Use punctuation (commas, parentheses, dashes) to set off nonrestrictive/ parenthetical elements.* b. Spell correctly.	2. Demonstrate command of the conventions of standard English capitalization, punctuation, and spelling when writing. a. Use a comma to separate coordinate adjectives (e.g., *It was a fascinating, enjoyable movie* but not *He wore an old[,] green shirt*). b. Spell correctly.	2. Demonstrate command of the conventions of standard English capitalization, punctuation, and spelling when writing. a. Use punctuation (comma, ellipsis, dash) to indicate a pause or break. b. Use an ellipsis to indicate an omission. c. Spell correctly.

		Grade 6 Students	Grade 7 Students	Grade 8 Students

Knowledge of Language		3. Use knowledge of language and its conventions when writing, speaking, reading, or listening.
		
		  a. Vary sentence patterns for meaning, reader/listener interest, and style.*
		
		  b. Maintain consistency in style and tone.*
			3. Use knowledge of language and its conventions when writing, speaking, reading, or listening.
			
			  a. Choose language that expresses ideas precisely and concisely, recognizing and eliminating wordiness and redundancy.*
				3. Use knowledge of language and its conventions when writing, speaking, reading, or listening.
				
				  a. Use verbs in the active and passive voice and in the conditional and subjunctive mood to achieve particular effects (e.g., emphasizing the actor or the action; expressing uncertainty or describing a state contrary to fact).

Vocabulary Acquisition and Use		4. Determine or clarify the meaning of unknown and multiple-meaning words and phrases based on *grade 6 reading and content,* choosing flexibly from a range of strategies.
		
		  a. Use context (e.g., the overall meaning of a sentence or paragraph; a word's position or function in a sentence) as a clue to the meaning of a word or phrase.
		
		  b. Use common, grade-appropriate Greek or Latin affixes and roots as clues to the meaning of a word (e.g., *audience, auditory, audible*).
		
		  c. Consult reference materials (e.g., dictionaries, glossaries, thesauruses), both print and digital, to find the pronunciation of a word or determine or clarify its precise meaning or its part of speech.
		
		  d. Verify the preliminary determination of the meaning of a word or phrase (e.g., by checking the inferred meaning in context or in a dictionary).
			4. Determine or clarify the meaning of unknown and multiple-meaning words and phrases based on *grade 7 reading and content,* choosing flexibly from a range of strategies.
			
			  a. Use context (e.g., the overall meaning of a sentence or paragraph; a word's position or function in a sentence) as a clue to the meaning of a word or phrase.
			
			  b. Use common, grade-appropriate Greek or Latin affixes and roots as clues to the meaning of a word (e.g., *belligerent, bellicose, rebel*).
			
			  c. Consult general and specialized reference materials (e.g., dictionaries, glossaries, thesauruses), both print and digital, to find the pronunciation of a word or determine or clarify its precise meaning or its part of speech **or trace the etymology of words. CA**
			
			  d. Verify the preliminary determination of the meaning of a word or phrase (e.g., by checking the inferred meaning in context or in a dictionary).
				4. Determine or clarify the meaning of unknown and multiple-meaning words or phrases based on *grade 8 reading and content,* choosing flexibly from a range of strategies.
				
				  a. Use context (e.g., the overall meaning of a sentence or paragraph; a word's position or function in a sentence) as a clue to the meaning of a word or phrase.
				
				  b. Use common, grade-appropriate Greek or Latin affixes and roots as clues to the meaning of a word (e.g., *precede, recede, secede*).
				
				  c. Consult general and specialized reference materials (e.g., dictionaries, glossaries, thesauruses), both print and digital, to find the pronunciation of a word or determine or clarify its precise meaning or its part of speech **or trace the etymology of words. CA**
				
				  d. Verify the preliminary determination of the meaning of a word or phrase (e.g., by checking the inferred meaning in context or in a dictionary).

	Grade 6 Students	Grade 7 Students	Grade 8 Students

Vocabulary Acquisition and Use (continued)	5. Demonstrate understanding of figurative language, word relationships, and nuances in word meanings.
	
	  a. Interpret figures of speech (e.g., personification) in context.
	
	  b. Use the relationship between particular words (e.g., cause/effect, part/whole, item/category) to better understand each of the words.
	
	  c. Distinguish among the connotations (associations) of words with similar denotations (definitions) (e.g., *stingy, scrimping, economical, unwasteful, thrifty*).
		5. Demonstrate understanding of figurative language, word relationships, and nuances in word meanings.
		
		  a. Interpret figures of speech (e.g., literary, biblical, and mythological allusions) in context.
		
		  b. Use the relationship between particular words (e.g., synonym/antonym, analogy) to better understand each of the words.
		
		  c. Distinguish among the connotations (associations) of words with similar denotations (definitions) (e.g., *refined, respectful, polite, diplomatic, condescending*).
			5. Demonstrate understanding of figurative language, word relationships, and nuances in word meanings.
			
			  a. Interpret figures of speech (e.g. verbal irony, puns) in context.
			
			  b. Use the relationship between particular words to better understand each of the words.
			
			  c. Distinguish among the connotations (associations) of words with similar denotations (definitions) (e.g., *bullheaded, willful, firm, persistent, resolute*).

	6. Acquire and use accurately grade-appropriate general academic and domain-specific words and phrases; gather vocabulary knowledge when considering a word or phrase important to comprehension or expression.	6. Acquire and use accurately grade-appropriate general academic and domain-specific words and phrases; gather vocabulary knowledge when considering a word or phrase important to comprehension or expression.	6. Acquire and use accurately grade-appropriate general academic and domain-specific words and phrases; gather vocabulary knowledge when considering a word or phrase important to comprehension or expression.

Language Standards 6–12

The CCR anchor standards and high school grade-specific standards work in tandem to define college and career readiness expectations—the former providing broad standards, the latter providing additional specificity.

Grades 9–10 Students	Grades 11–12 Students
Conventions of Standard English	

1. Demonstrate command of the conventions of standard English grammar and usage when writing or speaking.
 	
   a. Use parallel structure.*
 	
   b. Use various types of phrases (noun, verb, adjectival, adverbial, participial, prepositional, absolute) and clauses (independent, dependent; noun, relative, adverbial) to convey specific meanings and add variety and interest to writing or presentations.
	1. Demonstrate command of the conventions of standard English grammar and usage when writing or speaking.
	
	   a. Apply the understanding that usage is a matter of convention, can change over time, and is sometimes contested.
	
	   b. Resolve issues of complex or contested usage, consulting references (e.g., *Merriam-Webster's Dictionary of English Usage, Garner's Modern American Usage*) as needed.

2. Demonstrate command of the conventions of standard English capitalization, punctuation, and spelling when writing.
 	
   a. Use a semicolon (and perhaps a conjunctive adverb) to link two or more closely related independent clauses.
 	
   b. Use a colon to introduce a list or quotation.
 	
   c. Spell correctly.
	2. Demonstrate command of the conventions of standard English capitalization, punctuation, and spelling when writing.
	
	   a. Observe hyphenation conventions.
	
	   b. Spell correctly.

Knowledge of Language	

3. Apply knowledge of language to understand how language functions in different contexts, to make effective choices for meaning or style, and to comprehend more fully when reading or listening.
 	
   a. Write and edit work so that it conforms to the guidelines in a style manual (e.g., *MLA Handbook,* Turabian's *Manual for Writers*) appropriate for the discipline and writing type.
	3. Apply knowledge of language to understand how language functions in different contexts, to make effective choices for meaning or style, and to comprehend more fully when reading or listening.
	
	   a. Vary syntax for effect, consulting references (e.g., Tufte's *Artful Sentences*) for guidance as needed; apply an understanding of syntax to the study of complex texts when reading.

Grades 9–10 Students	Grades 11–12 Students
4. Determine or clarify the meaning of unknown and multiple-meaning words and phrases based on *grades 9–10 reading and content,* choosing flexibly from a range of strategies.	4. Determine or clarify the meaning of unknown and multiple-meaning words and phrases based on *grades 11–12 reading and content,* choosing flexibly from a range of strategies.
a. Use context (e.g., the overall meaning of a sentence, paragraph, or text; a word's position or function in a sentence) as a clue to the meaning of a word or phrase.	a. Use context (e.g., the overall meaning of a sentence, paragraph, or text; a word's position or function in a sentence) as a clue to the meaning of a word or phrase.
b. Identify and correctly use patterns of word changes that indicate different meanings or parts of speech (e.g., *analyze, analysis, analytical; advocate, advocacy*) **and continue to apply knowledge of Greek and Latin roots and affixes. CA**	b. Identify and correctly use patterns of word changes that indicate different meanings or parts of speech (e.g., *conceive, conception, conceivable*). **Apply knowledge of Greek, Latin, and Anglo-Saxon roots and affixes to draw inferences concerning the meaning of scientific and mathematical terminology. CA**
c. Consult general and specialized reference materials (e.g., **college-level dictionaries, rhyming dictionaries, bilingual dictionaries,** glossaries, thesauruses), both print and digital, to find the pronunciation of a word or determine or clarify its precise meaning, its part of speech, or its etymology. **CA**	c. Consult general and specialized reference materials (e.g., **college-level** dictionaries, **rhyming dictionaries, bilingual dictionaries,** glossaries, thesauruses), both print and digital, to find the pronunciation of a word or determine or clarify its precise meaning, its part of speech, its etymology, or its standard usage. **CA**
d. Verify the preliminary determination of the meaning of a word or phrase (e.g., by checking the inferred meaning in context or in a dictionary).	d. Verify the preliminary determination of the meaning of a word or phrase (e.g., by checking the inferred meaning in context or in a dictionary).
5. Demonstrate understanding of figurative language, word relationships, and nuances in word meanings.	5. Demonstrate understanding of figurative language, word relationships, and nuances in word meanings.
a. Interpret figures of speech (e.g., euphemism, oxymoron) in context and analyze their role in the text.	a. Interpret figures of speech (e.g., hyperbole, paradox) in context and analyze their role in the text.
b. Analyze nuances in the meaning of words with similar denotations.	b. Analyze nuances in the meaning of words with similar denotations.
6. Acquire and use accurately general academic and domain-specific words and phrases, sufficient for reading, writing, speaking, and listening at the college and career readiness level; demonstrate independence in gathering vocabulary knowledge when considering a word or phrase important to comprehension or expression.	6. Acquire and use accurately general academic and domain-specific words and phrases, sufficient for reading, writing, speaking, and listening at the college and career readiness level; demonstrate independence in gathering vocabulary knowledge when considering a word or phrase important to comprehension or expression.

Vocabulary Acquisition and Use

Language Progressive Skills, by Grade

The following skills, marked with an asterisk (*) in Language standards 1–3, are particularly likely to require continued attention in higher grades as they are applied to increasingly sophisticated writing and speaking.

Standard	Grade(s)							
	3	4	5	6	7	8	9–10	11–12
L.3.1f. Ensure subject-verb and pronoun-antecedent agreement.	Yes	Yes	Yes	Yes	Yes	Yes	Yes	Yes
L.3.3a. Choose words and phrases for effect.	Yes	Yes	Yes	Yes	Yes	Yes	Yes	Yes
L.4.1f. Produce complete sentences, recognizing and correcting inappropriate fragments and run-ons.	No	Yes	Yes	Yes	Yes	Yes	Yes	Yes
L.4.1g. Correctly use frequently confused words (e.g., *to/too/two; there/their*).	No	Yes	Yes	Yes	Yes	Yes	Yes	Yes
L.4.3a. Choose words and phrases to convey ideas precisely.*	No	Yes	Yes	Yes	No	No	No	No
L.4.3b. Choose punctuation for effect.	No	Yes	Yes	Yes	Yes	Yes	Yes	Yes
L.5.1d. Recognize and correct inappropriate shifts in verb tense.	No	No	Yes	Yes	Yes	Yes	Yes	Yes
L.5.2a. Use punctuation to separate items in a series.**	No	No	Yes	Yes	Yes	Yes	No	No
L.6.1c. Recognize and correct inappropriate shifts in pronoun number and person.	No	No	No	Yes	Yes	Yes	Yes	Yes
L.6.1d. Recognize and correct vague pronouns (i.e., ones with unclear or ambiguous antecedents).	No	No	No	Yes	Yes	Yes	Yes	Yes
L.6.1e. Recognize variations from standard English in their own and others' writing and speaking, and identify and use strategies to improve expression in conventional language.	No	No	No	Yes	Yes	Yes	Yes	Yes
L.6.2a. Use punctuation (commas, parentheses, dashes) to set off nonrestrictive/parenthetical elements.	No	No	No	Yes	Yes	Yes	Yes	Yes
L.6.3a. Vary sentence patterns for meaning, reader/listener interest, and style.***	No	No	No	Yes	Yes	Yes	Yes	No
L.6.3b. Maintain consistency in style and tone.	No	No	No	Yes	Yes	Yes	Yes	Yes
L.7.1c. Place phrases and clauses within a sentence, recognizing and correcting misplaced and dangling modifiers.	No	No	No	No	Yes	Yes	Yes	Yes
L.7.3a. Choose language that expresses ideas precisely and concisely, recognizing and eliminating wordiness and redundancy.	No	No	No	No	Yes	Yes	Yes	Yes
L.8.1d. Recognize and correct inappropriate shifts in verb voice and mood.	No	No	No	No	No	Yes	Yes	Yes
L.9–10.1a. Use parallel structure.	No	No	No	No	No	No	Yes	Yes

*Subsumed by L.7.3a.
**Subsumed by L.9–10.1a.
***Subsumed by L.11–12.3a.

Standard 10: Range, Quality, and Complexity of Student Reading 6–12

Measuring Text Complexity: Three Factors

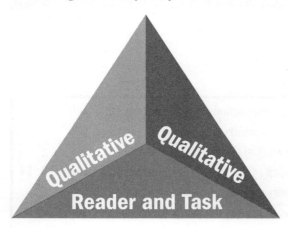

Qualitative

Qualitative

Reader and Task

Qualitative evaluation of the text:
Levels of meaning, structure, language conventionality and clarity, and knowledge demands

Quantitative evaluation of the text:
Readability measures and other scores of text complexity

Matching reader to text and task:
Reader variables (such as motivation, knowledge, and experiences) and task variables (such as purpose and the complexity generated by the task assigned and the questions posed)

Note: More detailed information on text complexity and how it is measured is provided in Appendix A.

Range of Text Types for 6–12

Students in grades 6–12 apply the Reading standards to the following range of text types, with texts selected from a broad range of cultures and periods.

Literature			Informational Text
Stories	**Drama**	**Poetry**	**Literary Nonfiction**
Includes the subgenres of adventure stories, historical fiction, mysteries, myths, science fiction, realistic fiction, allegories, parodies, satire, and graphic novels.	Includes **classical through contemporary** one-act and multi-act plays, both in written form and on film, **and works by writers representing a broad range of literary periods and cultures. CA**	Includes **classical through contemporary works and** the subgenres of narrative poems, lyrical poems, free verse poems, sonnets, odes, ballads, and epics **by writers representing a broad range of literary periods and cultures. CA**	Includes the subgenres of exposition, argument, and functional text in the form of personal essays, speeches, opinion pieces, essays about art or literature, biographies, memoirs, journalism, and historical, scientific, technical, or economic accounts (including digital sources) written for a broad audience.

Texts Illustrating the Complexity, Quality, and Range of Student Reading 6–12

	Literature: Stories, Dramas, Poetry	Informational Texts: Literary Nonfiction
6–8	<ul><li>*Little Women* by Louisa May Alcott (1869)</li><li>*The Adventures of Tom Sawyer* by Mark Twain (1876)</li><li>"The Road Not Taken" by Robert Frost (1915)</li><li>*The Dark Is Rising* by Susan Cooper (1973)</li><li>*Dragonwings* by Laurence Yep (1975)</li><li>*Roll of Thunder, Hear My Cry* by Mildred Taylor (1976)</li></ul>	<ul><li>"Letter on Thomas Jefferson" by John Adams (1776)</li><li>*Narrative of the Life of Frederick Douglass, an American Slave* by Frederick Douglass (1845)</li><li>"Blood, Toil, Tears and Sweat: Address to Parliament on May 13th, 1940" by Winston Churchill (1940)</li><li>*Harriet Tubman: Conductor on the Underground Railroad* by Ann Petry (1955)</li><li>*Travels with Charley: In Search of America* by John Steinbeck (1962)</li></ul>
9–10	<ul><li>*The Tragedy of Macbeth* by William Shakespeare (1592)</li><li>"Ozymandias" by Percy Bysshe Shelley (1817)</li><li>"The Raven" by Edgar Allen Poe (1845)</li><li>"The Gift of the Magi" by O. Henry (1906)</li><li>*The Grapes of Wrath* by John Steinbeck (1939)</li><li>*Fahrenheit 451* by Ray Bradbury (1953)</li><li>*The Killer Angels* by Michael Shaara (1975)</li></ul>	<ul><li>"Speech to the Second Virginia Convention" by Patrick Henry (1775)</li><li>"Farewell Address" by George Washington (1796)</li><li>"Gettysburg Address" by Abraham Lincoln (1863)</li><li>"State of the Union Address" by Franklin Delano Roosevelt (1941)</li><li>"Letter from Birmingham Jail" by Martin Luther King, Jr. (1964)</li><li>"Hope, Despair and Memory" by Elie Wiesel (1997)</li></ul>
11–CCR	<ul><li>"Ode on a Grecian Urn" by John Keats (1820)</li><li>*Jane Eyre* by Charlotte Brontë (1848)</li><li>"Because I Could Not Stop for Death" by Emily Dickinson (1890)</li><li>*The Great Gatsby* by F. Scott Fitzgerald (1925)</li><li>*Their Eyes Were Watching God* by Zora Neale Hurston (1937)</li><li>*A Raisin in the Sun* by Lorraine Hansberry (1959)</li><li>*The Namesake* by Jhumpa Lahiri (2003)</li></ul>	<ul><li>*Common Sense* by Thomas Paine (1776)</li><li>*Walden* by Henry David Thoreau (1854)</li><li>"Society and Solitude" by Ralph Waldo Emerson (1857)</li><li>"The Fallacy of Success" by G. K. Chesterton (1909)</li><li>*Black Boy* by Richard Wright (1945)</li><li>"Politics and the English Language" by George Orwell (1946)</li><li>"Take the Tortillas Out of Your Poetry" by Rudolfo Anaya (1995)</li></ul>

Note: Given space limitations, the illustrative texts listed above are meant only to show individual titles that are representative of a range of topics and genres. (See Appendix B for excerpts of these and other texts illustrative of grades 6–12 text complexity, quality, and range.) At a curricular or instructional level, within and across grade levels, texts need to be selected around topics or themes that generate knowledge and allow students to study those topics or themes in depth.

Standards for

Literacy in History/Social Studies, Science, and Technical Subjects

6–12

College and Career Readiness Anchor Standards for Reading

The grades 6–12 standards on the following pages define what students should understand and be able to do by the end of each grade. They correspond to the College and Career Readiness (CCR) anchor standards below by number. The CCR and grade-specific standards are necessary complements—the former providing broad standards, the latter providing additional specificity—that together define the skills and understandings that all students must demonstrate.

Key Ideas and Details

1. Read closely to determine what the text says explicitly and to make logical inferences from it; cite specific textual evidence when writing or speaking to support conclusions drawn from the text.

2. Determine central ideas or themes of a text and analyze their development; summarize the key supporting details and ideas.

3. Analyze how and why individuals, events, and ideas develop and interact over the course of a text.

Craft and Structure

4. Interpret words and phrases as they are used in a text, including determining technical, connotative, and figurative meanings, and analyze how specific word choices shape meaning or tone.

5. Analyze the structure of texts, including how specific sentences, paragraphs, and larger portions of the text (e.g., a section, chapter, scene, or stanza) relate to each other and the whole.

6. Assess how point of view or purpose shapes the content and style of a text.

Integration of Knowledge and Ideas

7. Integrate and evaluate content presented in diverse media and formats, including visually and quantitatively, as well as in words.*

*Please see "Research to Build and Present Knowledge" in Writing and "Comprehension and Collaboration" in Speaking and Listening for additional standards relevant to gathering, assessing, and applying information from print and digital sources.

8. Delineate and evaluate the argument and specific claims in a text, including the validity of the reasoning as well as the relevance and sufficiency of the evidence.

9. Analyze how two or more texts address similar themes or topics in order to build knowledge or to compare the approaches the authors take.

Range of Reading and Level of Text Complexity

10. Read and comprehend complex literary and informational texts independently and proficiently.

Note on range and content of student reading

Reading is critical to building knowledge in history/social studies as well as in science and technical subjects. College and career ready reading in these fields requires an appreciation of the norms and conventions of each discipline, such as the kinds of evidence used in history and science; an understanding of domain-specific words and phrases; an attention to precise details; and the capacity to evaluate intricate arguments, synthesize complex information, and follow detailed descriptions of events and concepts. In history/social studies, for example, students need to be able to analyze, evaluate, and differentiate primary and secondary sources. When reading scientific and technical texts, students need to be able to gain knowledge from challenging texts that often make extensive use of elaborate diagrams and data to convey information and illustrate concepts. Students must be able to read complex informational texts in these fields with independence and confidence because the vast majority of reading in college and workforce training programs will be sophisticated nonfiction. It is important to note that these Reading standards are meant to complement the specific content demands of the disciplines, not replace them.

Reading Standards for Literacy in History/Social Studies 6–12

The standards below begin at grade 6; standards for K–5 reading in history/social studies, science, and technical subjects are integrated into the K–5 Reading standards. The CCR anchor standards and high school standards in literacy work in tandem to define college and career readiness expectations—the former providing broad standards, the latter providing additional specificity.

	Grade 6–8 Students	Grade 9–10 Students	Grade 11–12 Students
Key Ideas and Details	1. Cite specific textual evidence to support analysis of primary and secondary sources.	1. Cite specific textual evidence to support analysis of primary and secondary sources, attending to such features as the date and origin of the information.	1. Cite specific textual evidence to support analysis of primary and secondary sources, connecting insights gained from specific details to an understanding of the text as a whole.
	2. Determine the central ideas or information of a primary or secondary source; provide an accurate summary of the source distinct from prior knowledge or opinions.	2. Determine the central ideas or information of a primary or secondary source; provide an accurate summary of how key events or ideas develop over the course of the text.	2. Determine the central ideas or information of a primary or secondary source; provide an accurate summary that makes clear the relationships among the key details and ideas.
	3. Identify key steps in a text's description of a process related to history/social studies (e.g., how a bill becomes law, how interest rates are raised or lowered).	3. Analyze in detail a series of events described in a text; determine whether earlier events caused later ones or simply preceded them.	3. Evaluate various explanations for actions or events and determine which explanation best accords with textual evidence, acknowledging where the text leaves matters uncertain.
Craft and Structure	4. Determine the meaning of words and phrases as they are used in a text, including vocabulary specific to domains related to history/social studies.	4. Determine the meaning of words and phrases as they are used in a text, including vocabulary describing political, social, or economic aspects of history/social science.	4. Determine the meaning of words and phrases as they are used in a text, including analyzing how an author uses and refines the meaning of a key term over the course of a text (e.g., how Madison defines *faction* in *Federalist* No. 10).
	5. Describe how a text presents information (e.g., sequentially, comparatively, causally).	5. Analyze how a text uses structure to emphasize key points or advance an explanation or analysis.	5. Analyze in detail how a complex primary source is structured, including how key sentences, paragraphs, and larger portions of the text contribute to the whole.
	6. Identify aspects of a text that reveal an author's point of view or purpose (e.g., loaded language, inclusion or avoidance of particular facts).	6. Compare the point of view of two or more authors for how they treat the same or similar topics, including which details they include and emphasize in their respective accounts.	6. Evaluate authors' differing points of view on the same historical event or issue by assessing the authors' claims, reasoning, and evidence.

		Grade 6–8 Students	Grade 9–10 Students	Grade 11–12 Students
Integration of Knowledge and Ideas	7.	Integrate visual information (e.g., in charts, graphs, photographs, videos, or maps) with other information in print and digital texts.	7. Integrate quantitative or technical analysis (e.g., charts, research data) with qualitative analysis in print or digital text.	7. Integrate and evaluate multiple sources of information presented in diverse formats and media (e.g., visually, quantitatively, as well as in words) in order to address a question or solve a problem.
	8.	Distinguish among fact, opinion, and reasoned judgment in a text.	8. Assess the extent to which the reasoning and evidence in a text support the author's claims.	8. Evaluate an author's premises, claims, and evidence by corroborating or challenging them with other information.
	9.	Analyze the relationship between a primary and secondary source on the same topic.	9. Compare and contrast treatments of the same topic in several primary and secondary sources.	9. Integrate information from diverse sources, both primary and secondary, into a coherent understanding of an idea or event, noting discrepancies among sources.
Range of Reading and Level of Text Complexity	10.	By the end of grade 8, read and comprehend history/social studies texts in the grades 6–8 text complexity band independently and proficiently.	10. By the end of grade 10, read and comprehend history/social studies texts in the grades 9–10 text complexity band independently and proficiently.	10. By the end of grade 12, read and comprehend history/social studies texts in the grades 11–12 text complexity band independently and proficiently.

Reading Standards for Literacy in Science and Technical Subjects 6–12

	Grade 6–8 Students	Grade 9–10 Students	Grade 11–12 Students
Key Ideas and Details	1. Cite specific textual evidence to support analysis of science and technical texts.	1. Cite specific textual evidence to support analysis of science and technical texts, attending to the precise details of explanations or descriptions.	1. Cite specific textual evidence to support analysis of science and technical texts, attending to important distinctions the author makes and to any gaps or inconsistencies in the account.
	2. Determine the central ideas or conclusions of a text; provide an accurate summary of the text distinct from prior knowledge or opinions.	2. Determine the central ideas or conclusions of a text; trace the text's explanation or depiction of a complex process, phenomenon, or concept; provide an accurate summary of the text.	2. Determine the central ideas or conclusions of a text; summarize complex concepts, processes, or information presented in a text by paraphrasing them in simpler but still accurate terms.
	3. Follow precisely a multistep procedure when carrying out experiments, taking measurements, or performing technical tasks.	3. Follow precisely a complex multistep procedure when carrying out experiments, taking measurements, or performing technical tasks, attending to special cases or exceptions defined in the text.	3. Follow precisely a complex multistep procedure when carrying out experiments, taking measurements, or performing technical tasks; analyze the specific results based on explanations in the text.
Craft and Structure	4. Determine the meaning of symbols, key terms, and other domain-specific words and phrases as they are used in a specific scientific or technical context relevant to *grades 6–8 texts and topics*.	4. Determine the meaning of symbols, key terms, and other domain-specific words and phrases as they are used in a specific scientific or technical context relevant to *grades 9–10 texts and topics*.	4. Determine the meaning of symbols, key terms, and other domain-specific words and phrases as they are used in a specific scientific or technical context relevant to *grades 11–12 texts and topics*.
	5. Analyze the structure an author uses to organize a text, including how the major sections contribute to the whole and to an understanding of the topic.	5. Analyze the structure of the relationships among concepts in a text, including relationships among key terms (e.g., *force, friction, reaction force, energy*).	5. Analyze how the text structures information or ideas into categories or hierarchies, demonstrating understanding of the information or ideas.
	6. Analyze the author's purpose in providing an explanation, describing a procedure, or discussing an experiment in a text.	6. Analyze the author's purpose in providing an explanation, describing a procedure, or discussing an experiment in a text, defining the question the author seeks to address.	6. Analyze the author's purpose in providing an explanation, describing a procedure, or discussing an experiment in a text, identifying important issues that remain unresolved.

	Grade 6–8 Students	Grade 9–10 Students	Grade 11–12 Students
Integration of Knowledge and Ideas	7. Integrate quantitative or technical information expressed in words in a text with a version of that information expressed visually (e.g., in a flowchart, diagram, model, graph, or table).	7. Translate quantitative or technical information expressed in words in a text into visual form (e.g., a table or chart) and translate information expressed visually or mathematically (e.g., in an equation) into words.	7. Integrate and evaluate multiple sources of information presented in diverse formats and media (e.g., quantitative data, video, multimedia) in order to address a question or solve a problem.
	8. Distinguish among facts, reasoned judgment based on research findings, and speculation in a text.	8. Assess the extent to which the reasoning and evidence in a text support the author's claim or a recommendation for solving a scientific or technical problem.	8. Evaluate the hypotheses, data, analysis, and conclusions in a science or technical text, verifying the data when possible and corroborating or challenging conclusions with other sources of information.
	9. Compare and contrast the information gained from experiments, simulations, video, or multimedia sources with that gained from reading a text on the same topic.	9. Compare and contrast findings presented in a text to those from other sources (including their own experiments), noting when the findings support or contradict previous explanations or accounts.	9. Synthesize information from a range of sources (e.g., texts, experiments, simulations) into a coherent understanding of a process, phenomenon, or concept, resolving conflicting information when possible.
Range of Reading and Level of Text Complexity	10. By the end of grade 8, read and comprehend science/technical texts in the grades 6–8 text complexity band independently and proficiently.	10. By the end of grade 10, read and comprehend science/technical texts in the grades 9–10 text complexity band independently and proficiently.	10. By the end of grade 12, read and comprehend science/technical texts in the grades 11–12 text complexity band independently and proficiently.

College and Career Readiness Anchor Standards for Writing

The grades 6–12 standards on the following pages define what students should understand and be able to do by the end of each grade. They correspond to the College and Career Readiness (CCR) anchor standards below by number. The CCR and grade-specific standards are necessary complements—the former providing broad standards, the latter providing additional specificity—that together define the skills and understandings that all students must demonstrate.

Text Types and Purposes*

1. Write arguments to support claims in an analysis of substantive topics or texts using valid reasoning and relevant and sufficient evidence.

2. Write informative/explanatory texts to examine and convey complex ideas and information clearly and accurately through the effective selection, organization, and analysis of content.

3. Write narratives to develop real or imagined experiences or events using effective technique, well-chosen details, and well-structured event sequences.

Production and Distribution of Writing

4. Produce clear and coherent writing in which the development, organization, and style are appropriate to task, purpose, and audience.

5. Develop and strengthen writing as needed by planning, revising, editing, rewriting, or trying a new approach.

6. Use technology, including the Internet, to produce and publish writing and to interact and collaborate with others.

Research to Build and Present Knowledge

7. Conduct short as well as more sustained research projects based on focused questions, demonstrating understanding of the subject under investigation.

*These broad types of writing include many subgenres. See Appendix A for definitions of key writing types.

8. Gather relevant information from multiple print and digital sources, assess the credibility and accuracy of each source, and integrate the information while avoiding plagiarism.

9. Draw evidence from literary and/or informational texts to support analysis, reflection, and research.

Range of Writing

10. Write routinely over extended time frames (time for research, reflection, and revision) and shorter time frames (a single sitting or a day or two) for a range of tasks, purposes, and audiences.

Note on range and content of student writing

For students, writing is a key means of asserting and defending claims, showing what they know about a subject, and conveying what they have experienced, imagined, thought, and felt. To be college and career ready writers, students must take task, purpose, and audience into careful consideration, choosing words, information, structures, and formats deliberately. They need to be able to use technology strategically when creating, refining, and collaborating on writing. They have to become adept at gathering information, evaluating sources, and citing material accurately, reporting findings from their research and analysis of sources in a clear and cogent manner. They must have the flexibility, concentration, and fluency to produce high-quality first-draft text under a tight deadline as well as the capacity to revisit and make improvements to a piece of writing over multiple drafts when circumstances encourage or require it. To meet these goals, students must devote significant time and effort to writing, producing numerous pieces over short and long time frames throughout the year.

Writing Standards for Literacy in History/Social Studies, Science, and Technical Subjects 6–12

The standards below begin at grade 6; standards for K–5 writing in history/social studies, science, and technical subjects are integrated into the K–5 Writing standards. The CCR anchor standards and high school standards in literacy work in tandem to define college and career readiness expectations—the former providing broad standards, the latter providing additional specificity.

Grade 6–8 Students	Grade 9–10 Students	Grade 11–12 Students

1. Write arguments focused on *discipline-specific content*.
 	
  a. Introduce claim(s) about a topic or issue, acknowledge and distinguish the claim(s) from alternate or opposing claims, and organize the reasons and evidence logically.
 	
  b. Support claim(s) with logical reasoning and relevant, accurate data and evidence that demonstrate an understanding of the topic or text, using credible sources.
 	
  c. Use words, phrases, and clauses to create cohesion and clarify the relationships among claim(s), counterclaims, reasons, and evidence.
 	
  d. Establish and maintain a formal style.
 	
  e. Provide a concluding statement or section that follows from and supports the argument presented.
	1. Write arguments focused on *discipline-specific content*.
	
	  a. Introduce precise claim(s), distinguish the claim(s) from alternate or opposing claims, and create an organization that establishes clear relationships among the claim(s), counterclaims, reasons, and evidence.
	
	  b. Develop claim(s) and counterclaims fairly, supplying data and evidence for each while pointing out the strengths and limitations of both claim(s) and counterclaims in a discipline-appropriate form and in a manner that anticipates the audience's knowledge level and concerns.
	
	  c. Use words, phrases, and clauses to link the major sections of the text, create cohesion, and clarify the relationships between claim(s) and reasons, between reasons and evidence, and between claim(s) and counterclaims.
	
	  d. Establish and maintain a formal style and objective tone while attending to the norms and conventions of the discipline in which they are writing.
	
	  e. Provide a concluding statement or section that follows from or supports the argument presented.
		1. Write arguments focused on *discipline-specific content*.
		
		  a. Introduce precise, knowledgeable claim(s), establish the significance of the claim(s), distinguish the claim(s) from alternate or opposing claims, and create an organization that logically sequences the claim(s), counterclaims, reasons, and evidence.
		
		  b. Develop claim(s) and counterclaims fairly and thoroughly, supplying the most relevant data and evidence for each while pointing out the strengths and limitations of both claim(s) and counterclaims in a discipline-appropriate form that anticipates the audience's knowledge level, concerns, values, and possible biases.
		
		  c. Use words, phrases, and clauses as well as varied syntax to link the major sections of the text, create cohesion, and clarify the relationships between claim(s) and reasons, between reasons and evidence, and between claim(s) and counterclaims.
		
		  d. Establish and maintain a formal style and objective tone while attending to the norms and conventions of the discipline in which they are writing.
		
		  e. Provide a concluding statement or section that follows from or supports the argument presented.

Text Types and Purposes

Grade 6–8 Students	Grade 9–10 Students	Grade 11–12 Students
2. Write informative/explanatory texts, including the narration of historical events, scientific procedures/experiments, or technical processes. a. Introduce a topic clearly, previewing what is to follow; organize ideas, concepts, and information into broader categories as appropriate to achieving purpose; include formatting (e.g., headings), graphics (e.g., charts, tables), and multimedia when useful to aiding comprehension. b. Develop the topic with relevant, well-chosen facts, definitions, concrete details, quotations, or other information and examples. c. Use appropriate and varied transitions to create cohesion and clarify the relationships among ideas and concepts. d. Use precise language and domain-specific vocabulary to inform about or explain the topic. e. Establish and maintain a formal style and objective tone. f. Provide a concluding statement or section that follows from and supports the information or explanation presented.	2. Write informative/explanatory texts, including the narration of historical events, scientific procedures/experiments, or technical processes. a. Introduce a topic and organize ideas, concepts, and information to make important connections and distinctions; include formatting (e.g., headings), graphics (e.g., figures, tables), and multimedia when useful to aiding comprehension. b. Develop the topic with well-chosen, relevant, and sufficient facts, extended definitions, concrete details, quotations, or other information and examples appropriate to the audience's knowledge of the topic. c. Use varied transitions and sentence structures to link the major sections of the text, create cohesion, and clarify the relationships among ideas and concepts. d. Use precise language and domain-specific vocabulary to manage the complexity of the topic and convey a style appropriate to the discipline and context as well as to the expertise of likely readers. e. Establish and maintain a formal style and objective tone while attending to the norms and conventions of the discipline in which they are writing. f. Provide a concluding statement or section that follows from and supports the information or explanation presented (e.g., articulating implications or the significance of the topic).	2. Write informative/explanatory texts, including the narration of historical events, scientific procedures/experiments, or technical processes. a. Introduce a topic and organize complex ideas, concepts, and information so that each new element builds on that which precedes it to create a unified whole; include formatting (e.g., headings), graphics (e.g., figures, tables), and multimedia when useful to aiding comprehension. b. Develop the topic thoroughly by selecting the most significant and relevant facts, extended definitions, concrete details, quotations, or other information and examples appropriate to the audience's knowledge of the topic. c. Use varied transitions and sentence structures to link the major sections of the text, create cohesion, and clarify the relationships among complex ideas and concepts. d. Use precise language, domain-specific vocabulary and techniques such as metaphor, simile, and analogy to manage the complexity of the topic; convey a knowledgeable stance in a style that responds to the discipline and context as well as to the expertise of likely readers. e. Provide a concluding statement or section that follows from and supports the information or explanation provided (e.g., articulating implications or the significance of the topic).
3. (See note; not applicable as a separate requirement)	3. (See note; not applicable as a separate requirement)	3. (See note; not applicable as a separate requirement)

The leftmost column has a vertical label: **Text Types and Purposes (continued)**

	Grade 6–8 Students	Grade 9–10 Students	Grade 11–12 Students
Production and Distribution of Writing	4. Produce clear and coherent writing in which the development, organization, and style are appropriate to task, purpose, and audience.	4. Produce clear and coherent writing in which the development, organization, and style are appropriate to task, purpose, and audience.	4. Produce clear and coherent writing in which the development, organization, and style are appropriate to task, purpose, and audience.
	5. With some guidance and support from peers and adults, develop and strengthen writing as needed by planning, revising, editing, rewriting, or trying a new approach, focusing on how well purpose and audience have been addressed.	5. Develop and strengthen writing as needed by planning, revising, editing, rewriting, or trying a new approach, focusing on addressing what is most significant for a specific purpose and audience.	5. Develop and strengthen writing as needed by planning, revising, editing, rewriting, or trying a new approach, focusing on addressing what is most significant for a specific purpose and audience.
	6. Use technology, including the Internet, to produce and publish writing and present the relationships between information and ideas clearly and efficiently.	6. Use technology, including the Internet, to produce, publish, and update individual or shared writing products, taking advantage of technology's capacity to link to other information and to display information flexibly and dynamically.	6. Use technology, including the Internet, to produce, publish, and update individual or shared writing products in response to ongoing feedback, including new arguments or information.
Research to Build and Present Knowledge	7. Conduct short research projects to answer a question (including a self-generated question), drawing on several sources and generating additional related, focused questions that allow for multiple avenues of exploration.	7. Conduct short as well as more sustained research projects to answer a question (including a self-generated question) or solve a problem; narrow or broaden the inquiry when appropriate; synthesize multiple sources on the subject, demonstrating understanding of the subject under investigation.	7. Conduct short as well as more sustained research projects to answer a question (including a self-generated question) or solve a problem; narrow or broaden the inquiry when appropriate; synthesize multiple sources on the subject, demonstrating understanding of the subject under investigation.

Note: Students' narrative skills continue to grow in these grades. The Standards require that students be able to incorporate narrative elements effectively into arguments and informative/explanatory texts. In history/social studies, students must be able to incorporate narrative accounts into their analyses of individuals or events of historical import. In science and technical subjects, students must be able to write precise enough descriptions of the step-by-step procedures they use in their investigations or technical work that others can replicate them and (possibly) reach the same results.

	Grade 6–8 Students	Grade 9–10 Students	Grade 11–12 Students
Research to Build and Present Knowledge (continued)	8. Gather relevant information from multiple print and digital sources **(primary and secondary)**, using search terms effectively; assess the credibility and accuracy of each source; and quote or paraphrase the data and conclusions of others while avoiding plagiarism and following a standard format for citation. **CA**	8. Gather relevant information from multiple authoritative print and digital sources **(primary and secondary)**, using advanced searches effectively; assess the usefulness of each source in answering the research question; integrate information into the text selectively to maintain the flow of ideas, avoiding plagiarism and following a standard format for citation. **CA**	8. Gather relevant information from multiple authoritative print and digital sources, using advanced searches effectively; assess the strengths and limitations of each source in terms of the specific task, purpose, and audience; integrate information into the text selectively to maintain the flow of ideas, avoiding plagiarism and overreliance on any one source and following a standard format for citation.
	9. Draw evidence from informational texts to support analysis reflection, and research.	9. Draw evidence from informational texts to support analysis, reflection, and research.	9. Draw evidence from informational texts to support analysis, reflection, and research.
Range of Writing	10. Write routinely over extended time frames (time for reflection and revision) and shorter time frames (a single sitting or a day or two) for a range of discipline-specific tasks, purposes, and audiences.	10. Write routinely over extended time frames (time for reflection and revision) and shorter time frames (a single sitting or a day or two) for a range of discipline-specific tasks, purposes, and audiences.	10. Write routinely over extended time frames (time for reflection and revision) and shorter time frames (a single sitting or a day or two) for a range of discipline-specific tasks, purposes, and audiences.

12-012 PR13-0002 7-13 10,000   OSP 13 131210